Ger

Radical Futures series

Hilary Wainwright, *A New Politics from the Left*
Graham Jones, *The Shock Doctrine of the Left*
Gianpaolo Baiocchi, *We, the Sovereign*
Keir Milburn, *Generation Left*

Keir Milburn

———————

Generation Left

polity

Copyright © Keir Milburn 2019

The right of Keir Milburn to be identified as Author of this Work has been asserted in accordance with the UK Copyright, Designs and Patents Act 1988.

First published in 2019 by Polity Press

Polity Press
65 Bridge Street
Cambridge CB2 1UR, UK

Polity Press
101 Station Landing
Suite 300
Medford, MA 02155, USA

ISBN-13: 978-1-5095-3223-0
ISBN-13: 978-1-5095-3224-7 (pb)

A catalogue record for this book is available from the British Library.

Library of Congress Cataloging-in-Publication Data
Names: Milburn, Keir, author.
Title: Generation left / Keir Milburn.
Description: Cambridge, UK ; Medford, MA, USA : Polity Press, 2019. | Series: Radical futures | Includes bibliographical references and index.
Identifiers: LCCN 2018050590 (print) | LCCN 2019000291 (ebook) | ISBN 9781509532261 (Epub) | ISBN 9781509532230 | ISBN 9781509532247 (pb)
Subjects: LCSH: Right and left (Political science) | Young adults--Political activity. | Generations--Political aspects. | Age--Political aspects.
Classification: LCC JA83 (ebook) | LCC JA83 .M55 2019 (print) | DDC 320.53--dc23
LC record available at https://lccn.loc.gov/2018050590

Typeset in 11 on 15 Sabon by Servis Filmsetting Ltd, Stockport, Cheshire
Printed and bound in Great Britain by CPI Group (UK) Ltd, Croydon

For further information on Polity, visit our website: politybooks.com

Contents

Acknowledgements

Theory is never simply generated by individuals. At best, authors immerse themselves in the general intellect of their times, find new ways of articulating the problems that social movements are struggling with and suggest avenues for addressing them. Out of that general intellect there are several people I'd like to thank. Firstly, my thanks go to my editors at Polity, George Owers and Julia Davies, for both their patience and their thoughtful editorial suggestions. I also want to thank Rodrigo Nunes and Bue Rubner Hansen for commenting on drafts of the book. Huge thanks go to my comrades in Plan C who have helped frame the problems with which I've engaged since 2011 and provided the invaluable lessons that come with attempting to address them practically. Over the last year or so I've also participated in the Acid Joy Collective, whose discussions

Acknowledgements

have both raised my consciousness and helped me think through the electoral turn. Many of the ideas in this book have been incubated for a long time after getting their first development within the collective writing project The Free Association. In particular, I'd like to thank members David Harvie and Brian Lyang, who, along with Gareth Brown, have influenced my thinking and helped frame the conceptual assemblage in the book the most. Last but not least, my thanks go to Alice Nutter and Mae Rose Milburn not just for being supportive but also for being good fun.

Each generation must, out of relative obscurity, discover its mission, fulfill it, or betray it.

Frantz Fanon

The storms of youth precede brilliant days.

Comte de Lautréamont

1

Re: Generations

Something remarkable has happened over the last few years. Age has emerged as the key dividing line in politics. Young people are much more likely to vote Left and hold left-wing views, while older generations are more likely to vote Right and hold conservative social, and increasingly political, views. This pattern isn't universal, but it holds true across the US, the UK and much of Western Europe. The scale of the divide is unprecedented, and although it's begun to attract attention, its political significance has been overlooked. Much existing analysis has simply accepted existing conceptions of what political generations are and how they are formed. Those ideas might have suited the generation gap of the 1960s and 1970s, when they were developed, but they don't fit the current situation. Our generation gap has its own characteristics and needs a new concept of political generations to capture them. We need to understand how the young are reshaping the Left to accord with their experiences and desires. A generation moving left is producing a new generation of Left ideas and practices. It's a phenomenon that's currently among the most important in the world to grasp.

This book traces the emergence of Generation Left through two international waves of development: the protest wave of 2011 and the electoral turn in the years that followed. At first glance these waves seem contradictory, but the continuities show a generation in continuing development. The economic crisis of 2008 is the key event of our time. It has crystallized and accelerated the ongoing generational divide in life chances. As young people, among others, found their conditions of life increasingly intolerable, they began a process of identifying and rejecting the structural constraints placed upon them. Generational dynamics of political inheritance and supersession are determining this process. We find ourselves living in one of those rare moments when history opens up. We face exhilarating possibilities but also terrifying threats. The rise of the Far Right and the consequences of climate change loom over our time like a nightmare. Yet the potential for a decisive move towards equality and freedom is greater than at any time in the past 40 years. The outcome of the political battles fought now will likely set the direction for the decades to come. The stakes for Generation Left really couldn't be higher.

Youth Turn Left

Through the summer of 2017 the phrase 'Oh, Jeremy Corbyn', chanted to the tune of the White Stripes song 'Seven Nation Army', echoed around high streets, pubs and music festivals up and down the UK. It was the sonic embodiment of the UK's political generation gap in all its anomalies. The dramatic increase in youth support for the Labour Party in the June general election that year became encapsulated in the unlikely figure of Jeremy Corbyn, a mild-mannered 68-year-old leftist, and recently elected party leader. The emergence of age as the key indicator of voting intention in the UK has been sudden and emphatic. On election day Labour had a 54 per cent lead over the Conservatives among 18- to 24-year-olds while the Conservatives led Labour by 35 points among the over 65s.[1] In a much-repeated statistic the polling firm YouGov showed the likelihood of voting Conservative went up 9 per cent for every 10 years older you were. There was an amazing 97 percentage point gap in voting intention between youngest and oldest voters. This division was not only historically unprecedented, it had also opened up quickly. At the 2010 general election the gap had been just 15 points.[2]

In the US, the political generation gap was seen most clearly during the race to be Democratic Party candidate for the 2016 Presidential election. Senator Bernie Sanders, at the time the only member of Congress to self-identify as a socialist, surprised everyone by taking his opponent Hillary Clinton to the wire. Not only was the Sanders campaign driven by the activism and votes of young people, but astoundingly, considering the prospect of the first female US president, the biggest cleavage in voting intentions fell not on gender, race or class, but on age. The numbers are stark. Sanders gained 72 per cent of 17- to 29-year-old votes while Clinton received just 28 per cent. At the other end of the age scale the division was almost exactly reversed, with Clinton gaining 71 per cent of the over 65 vote, while Sanders got just 27 per cent. So dominant was Sanders among the youth that he gained more under 30 votes than both Clinton and Trump combined.[3]

In April 2016 a leading US polling expert, John Della Volpe, declared that the Bernie Sanders campaign was not just 'moving a party to the left' but 'moving a generation to the left'. 'Whether or not he's winning or losing,' explained Della Volpe, 'he's impacting the way in which a generation – the largest generation in the history of America – thinks about politics.'[4] It was a conclusion reached via that year's iteration of the Harvard Institute of Politics' annual poll of young people, which showed the uptake of a whole series of opinions associated with left-wing views. Foremost among these were the changing attitudes towards the idea of socialism, with 33 per cent of 18- to 29-year-olds looking favourably on that word while a majority rejected capitalism.[5] By contrast a 2015 poll showed that those over 65, and so raised during the Cold War era, had very different views, with 59 per cent favouring capitalism and only 15 per cent declaring a favourable attitude towards socialism.[6]

It's likely, however, that Della Volpe is overstating the role of the Sanders campaign. Such moments act as trigger points, registering and accelerating trends that are already underway. In the US this acceleration is most easily seen through the post-Sanders growth of the Democratic Socialists of America (DSA), a left-wing organization whose members run on Democratic Party slates. In June 2016 the DSA had just 6,500 members; by September

2018 this had risen to 50,000, while the average age of members had dropped from 68 in 2013 to 33 in 2017. Then came the victory of 28-year-old DSA member Alexandria Ocasio-Cortez, who beat 18-year incumbent Joe Crowley in the 2018 Democratic Party primary for a New York seat at Congress. This astonishing victory, which was overwhelmingly driven by young voters, reflected a wave of left-wing primary and election victories around the country. By September 2018, 48 per cent of Democrat-supporting 'Millennials' (aged 22–37) were now calling themselves either socialist or democratic socialist.[7] It's a story repeated internationally. Youth support has been key to a wave of left-wing electoral projects in a variety of countries, from SYRIZA in Greece to Podemos in Spain. The near-simultaneity of the shift across different national contexts should indicate an underlying cause that goes beyond national political systems.

This hasn't been the only political upheaval in recent years. The ultimate shock of 2016 was the election of Donald Trump, and in the contest between Trump and Clinton the political cleavage amongst age cohorts was much less distinct. While Clinton beat Trump among younger voters, she saw a large decline from the level of youth vote gained by Obama. The youth who were enthused by the leftism of Sanders were left cold by Clinton's neo-liberal centrism. But while younger generations are deserting the centre, they aren't moving universally to the Left. In Eastern European countries, such as Hungary and Poland, a national swing to the Right and Far Right has been mirrored, not countered, by the votes of the youth. So how do we account for this general, but not universal, move to the Left among the young?

Generation Snowflake or Generation Screwed?

Our attempt to understand the young's new propensity for left-wing politics doesn't start from a blank page. There are already two incompatible narratives surrounding what gets called the 'Millennial' generation. The first casts Millennials as 'Generation Snowflake', who vote Left because they can't face the harsh realities of life. This right-wing narrative, which dominates in the mass media, often takes on preposterous dimensions. Millennials have taken the blame for everything, from the decline of the napkin industry to the fall of the nuclear family. The central assertion casts Millennials as over-entitled, indeed the most entitled generation in history, making unreasonable demands for a lifestyle they won't work for. This story is supplemented by the image of them as preening narcissists pushing themselves forwards for unearned recognition and reward. It's a narrative codified in books such as *Not Everyone Gets a Trophy* by Bruce Tulgan, and *Generation Me* by Jean Twenge.[8] Millennials, the argument goes, have been coddled into precious snowflakes who can't accept a challenge to their views. These same clichés are repeated *ad infinitum* by the commentators and talking heads of the media. Only such bludgeoning repetition could raise the 'safe space' policies of small student groups into the vital political problem of our times.

Yet alongside this story sits another description of Millennials in which, far from being coddled, they are being royally screwed over. In the UK Millennials are likely to be the first generation for hundreds of years who will earn less than the two generations who came before. This isn't just a prediction. It's already evident. By 2016 the average Millennial working through their twenties had already earnt £8,000 less than the average of the preceding generation.[9] The huge increase in house prices through the 1990s and 2000s was of benefit primarily to older generations. Declining wages, which have hit the young much more severely, along with post-crisis tightening of borrowing conditions, have put home ownership well out of reach of most young people. The result is a Generation Rent, who will spend 'an average of £44,000 more on rent in their 20s than baby boomers did'.[10] To make matters worse, young people are taking on huge sums of student debt only to discover a chronic shortage in graduate-level jobs. While some of these are long-term trends the situation has been massively accelerated by the economic crisis. In the UK 'all of the £2.7 trillion increase in aggregate wealth recorded since 2007 can be accounted for by the over-45s, with two-thirds accruing to the over-65s. In contrast, wealth has fallen by around 10 per cent among those aged 16–34.'[11]

The dimensions of this generational injustice aren't seriously disputed. So, how can we account for the persistent myth of over-entitlement? On one level, the discourse is designed to do ideological work on the young. During a period of declining wages, welfare rights and living standards, stories that chip away at young people's expectations are useful to the Right. But the Generation Snowflake stories are not really aimed at the young. They are best seen as self-justifying and comforting morality tales for the wealthier sections of older generations. They allow a sublimated accommodation with a disastrous economic situation of which they have, on average, been relative beneficiaries. Yet if that's what gives the narratives their attraction, they are held together by something else, a very specific, and actually quite odd, theory of how generational differences come about.

Right-wing commentators have been repeating the same moral panics about Millennials for over a decade, and the template for the story was laid down way before that. In fact the character of Generation Snowflake was established before there was any Millennial behaviour to provoke it. Neil Howe and William Strauss coined the term Millennial in their 1991 book *Generations: The History of America's Future, 1584 to 2069*. In this and in subsequent books the two ex-Congressional staffers and amateur historians lay out a fatalistic theory in which history is dominated by a generational pattern, a cycle of four archetypes that subsequent generations adopt: artists, prophets, nomads and heroes. They claim to have traced this cycle back to the American War of Independence and have mapped the character of future generations up to the year 2069.[12] This preposterous schema, which has been unjustifiably influential, functions like a horoscope. The vagueness of Howe and Strauss's claims allows the confirmation of pre-existing prejudices. In their 2000 book *Millennials Rising* they apply their model to Millennials, which they define as everyone born between 1982 and 2003. All who fall within this definition, including many not born at the time of publication, are destined to be part of a hero generation. 'They're optimists. . . . They're cooperative team players. . . . They accept authority. . . . They're rule followers. . . . They're the most watched over generation in memory. . . . Today's kids believe in the future and see themselves as its cutting edge.'[13] Most of the authors' claims about the Millennial character failed to survive the 2008 financial crisis, but the one about an over-protected generation did. That's because it's central to their idea of what generations are and how they are produced.

For Howe and Strauss, the generational cycle, and therefore the arc of history, is determined by oscillations in the dominant styles of childcare. 'Shared experiences' in childhood set the mode through which each generation reacts to the character failings of other generations as they move through stages of life. Generation Xers, neglected by their own Baby Boomer parents, have become, as they were destined to, over-protective parents. On the face of it this childrearing determinism, in which parenting styles are universalized and abstracted from other historical dynamics, makes little sense, and the evidence offered by Howe and

Strauss to back it up is laughable. But the prevailing ideology of the time offers few other avenues for explanations. If, as in the neoliberal world-view, the only natural social units are freely contracting individuals and family units – remember that, according to Margaret Thatcher, there is no such thing as society,[14] then there are very few variables with which to account for group phenomena. An explanation of generational difference caused by varying family structures fits the bill. But if this account of generations is unconvincing, what other accounts are out there?

What Generates a Generation?

Generally, when people talk about generations, in reference to societies rather than individual families, they're referring to all those born within roughly a 20-year period. If we assume that child-rearing age lasts around 20 years, let's say from 18 to 38, and note that birth to childrearing age has a somewhat similar span, then the logic is easy to see, but there's a problem here. Births take place continuously, each and every day, so how do you determine when one generation ends and another starts? It is usually assumed that one generation follows another in a sequential order. If we accept this sequentiality, and reject theories of trans-historic patterns of parenting, then we are led to the idea that generations must be endogenously generated through demographic dynamics. Birth rates vary and so generations can be aligned with either particularly large or particularly small age cohorts. For example, in its report *Stagnation Generation*, the Resolution Foundation, a think tank concerned with intergenerational justice, outlines four postwar generations: the Baby Boomers, born 1946–65; Generation X, born 1966–80; the Millennials, born 1981–2000; and an as yet unnamed generation, born 2001–15.[15] These do follow a rough oscillation between larger and smaller cohorts, but there is disagreement about when these generations begin and end.

This indeterminacy should give us pause for thought. Let's step back. Generational differences are not always prominent. The last time a generation gap was presented as a dominant political issue was during the 1960s and 1970s, when it primarily referred to a gap in cultural values. The size of the large Baby Boomer age cohort, who were coming of age at that time, allowed a distinct youth culture to emerge and demand attention. In fact, the Baby Boomers do fit with a conception of generations as endogenously generated by demographic changes. They are a large age cohort produced by a sudden and significant increase in birth rates, which then dropped off, suddenly and significantly, 20 years later. Yet if we dig a little deeper, even this example comes into doubt. The boundaries of the Baby Boomer cohort are clearly marked out by two events with dramatic demographic consequences. Its beginning is marked by the post-Second World War boom in the birth rate, while its end is marked by the introduction of the contraceptive pill. As these two events occurred roughly simultaneously across most of the developed world, they explain the common demographic bulge seen across different countries. But the bookending events of the Baby Boomers have causes that lay outside any continuing pattern of sequential generations. It seems hard to argue, for example, that the invention and roll-out of the contraceptive pill was caused by the size of the then current age cohort. Similarly, the Second World War and its end had a complex range of causes to which birth rates seem tangential. These events have demographic consequences not causes.

From this we can make two points. Firstly, and most straightforwardly, assigning generational differences to birth rates risks obscuring wider social, and indeed technological, causes. The second claim goes further. I think the very idea that generations are defined by changes in birth rates is the product of the Baby Boomer experience. It's the one generation that it actually seems to fit. In fact, that concept of generations is really just a Boomer's echo, applied to subsequent cohorts despite the marginal importance of generational differences to them. The concept loses coherence the further it moves from its point of origin. Our present period has a generation gap of a very different kind and it needs a different concept of generations to account for it. We can test this hypothesis by examining the causes of the current socio-economic and political generation gap and asking if the relative size of age cohorts underlies it.

What Generated This Generation?

In 2010 David Willetts, then UK Conservative Minister for Universities and Science, released an influential book on intergenerational justice called *The Pinch*.[16] In it he argues that the current generational gap in living standards is caused by the Baby Boomers being a large enough generation to change policy in their favour. Similarly, Ed Howker and

Re: Generations

Shiv Malik's 2013 book *Jilted Generation* points to greater voter turnout among older generations. But differences in generational sizes and turnouts is not new. Why is it that age has only recently become a key political indicator? Howker and Malik also blame five-year electoral cycles along with 'pollsters and analysts', and 'financial markets ... obsessed with rapid returns'. These, they argue, produce a 'natural tendency' towards short-term thinking in democratic governments which comes at the expense of the young.[17] The *Stagnation Generation* report cited above suggests 'baby boomers were just lucky, getting into the housing market and company pension schemes at the right time'.[18] But what caused house prices to rise? Why have financial markets grown more powerful? Why has the influence of pollsters and analysts increased while active mass democracy has declined? Is all this just chance as well?

What these explanations don't account for, and indeed seem ideologically predisposed not to see, is the role played by the 2008 economic crisis. The fall-out from 2008 caused the rapid change in economic circumstances that underlies the generation gap. But more than that, the event marks something epochal: the breaking of the neoliberal economic settlement. Actually existing neoliberalism, which emerged out of the previous epochal crisis in the 1970s, has delivered a 40-year stagnation in real wages.[19] The decline in union rights and membership, the principal cause of the falling wage, has been just one part of a wider hollowing out of democracy.[20] In compensation the implicit neoliberal deal offered the maintenance of living standards through cheaper goods and bountiful borrowing. As production followed low wages to the Global South, the price of consumer goods fell. Yet the developed world remained the global consumer of last resort. In a time of falling wages it was only access to cheap credit, underwritten by rising house prices, that allowed increased consumption. It is no coincidence that the unravelling began with a crisis in the housing market.

The long-term trends beneath the generation gap mark are an effect of a harshening neoliberal settlement. As conditions of work and social reproduction have worsened over time, they have affected later cohorts more severely. Older generations were employed on better terms and conditions, retained better pension rights and benefited from rising house prices that followed neoliberal reforms of the housing market. The crisis of 2008 caused these trends to accelerate, but more importantly it destroyed a key pillar of the deal: aspiration, the

17

expectations that living standards will improve, if not for you, then for your children.

Events Form Generations

If we want a concept of political generations that can include consideration of events such as 2008, then we can go back to Karl Mannheim's 1923 essay 'The Problem of Generations', which marks the birth of serious sociological thinking on the topic. For Mannheim generational divisions aren't something that happens sequentially or cyclically; they only emerge when, 'as a result of an acceleration in the tempo of social and cultural transformation basic attitudes must change so quickly that the latent, continuous adaptation and modification of traditional patterns of experience, thought and expression is no longer possible'.[21] This presents another problem. We live in a time in which the pace of change seems vertiginous, but much of this change is inconsequential: an update of the iPhone, a new film in the *Star Wars* franchise. We get the impression, to paraphrase Lampedusa, that everything is changing so that everything can stay the same. If we want to distinguish between this sort of change and the kind that can generate a generation, then we can use the concept of the 'event' as it is employed in contemporary critical theory.

The 'event' has long been a focus for modern philosophy, explored by, among others, Louis Althusser, Gilles Deleuze and Alain Badiou. While there are many differences between their ideas, we can still usefully define the event as a moment of sudden and unpredictable change that ruptures society's sense making. Events disrupt the stories that a society tells about itself; they disrupt the way a society makes sense of itself. They appear to come out of nowhere and change the direction change was previously moving in because they change 'the very parameter by which we measure the facts of change'.[22] Mannheim seems to have this level of transformation in mind when he links generations to 'the social and intellectual symptoms of a process of dynamic de-stabilization'.[23]

According to Mannheim, older people will encounter difficulties accepting the rupture of an event owing to our propensity to interpret new events through our own formative experiences, which 'tend to coalesce into a natural view of the world'.[24] The young, on the other hand, lacking a solidified interpretive prism formed of past experience, get 'fresh contact' with the problems the event produces and so get closer to them. Generational distinctions emerge if there are significant differences in the intellectual and psychic resources with which age cohorts encounter these events. The literature on events might loosen the connection between generations and age. Firstly, events occur at different scales. A really significant event might well force a reassessment even from those with an existing interpretive grid. Secondly, a political event that occurs in a particularly de-politicized period might widen the range of people open to something like a 'fresh contact' with its impact owing to the absence of firm political views. Indeed, Mannheim explains that 'certain impulses particular to a generation may, if the trend of the times is favourable to them, also attract individual members of earlier or later age-groups'.[25]

A major event gives those open to it what Mannheim calls a shared generational location, but it doesn't, on its own, determine the meaning of the event or the new sense it might produce. The event is a moment of de-stabilization; it may pose new problems, but it doesn't, on its own, produce a coherent political project or direction. Instead, Mannheim argues, different 'generational units' form around attempts to 'work up the material of their common experiences in different specific ways'. If the conditions are right, and the event is of a big enough magnitude, these units will try to hegemonize the wider generation by providing 'a more or less adequate expression of the particular "location" of a generation as a whole'.[26] The emergence of a generation involves the exploration of the problem space produced by the formative event.[27] This is the mission that Frantz Fanon says '[e]ach generation must' either 'fulfill ... or betray'.[28] This way of conceiving of generations helps us grasp the role of 2008, which crystallized long-term trends of intergenerational injustice into a generation-forming period of rapid change. But the current generation gap was produced by the different material resources with which age cohorts encountered the event as much as by their differing intellectual resources. The current generation gap is marked by diverging living standards, life chances, income and wealth. We already have a category for talking about such things. It's called class. So why does the divide show up around age?

In the UK, polling companies use the NRS (National Readership Survey) social grade system as a stand-in for class. Its categories, established to aid market research over 50 years ago, relate to a pattern of class formation that no longer exists. By categorizing manual workers as working class and non-manual workers as middle class, by failing to take account of income levels, job security or ownership of wealth, it fails to capture contemporary experience. Any analysis that tells us call-centre workers are middle class can't be taken seriously. Owing to changes in the labour market, manual workers tend to be older while young workers are more likely to do symbolic analysis, care work or other types of service work. This means that when class shows up in political polling it often serves as a proxy for age.[29]

To paraphrase Stuart Hall, age is currently one of the key modalities through which class is lived. It's the modality through which young people are becoming aware of their actual class position. But age also represents a fracture that makes the recognition of mutual class interests between the young and the old more difficult. And if class is fractured by age, then age cohorts are fractured by class divisions. A 2016 report from the British Department of Work and Pensions, for instance, showed a quarter of pensioners don't own their own home, while 1.6 million live in poverty. These complexities aren't revealed by the NRS social grade schema. We need a conception of class that can recognize changing class composition, as new class fractures develop and produce moments of non-communication. To capture these dynamics, while orienting to overcoming these barriers, we can turn to class composition analysis, but we will need to re-read that tradition in the light of Mannheim's theory of generations. These theories are compatible, I will argue, because class composition analysis was provoked by an instance of generational political miscommunication. As this conceptual combination of generational and class analysis will set the framework for the rest of the book, it's worth taking a little time over.

How Class is Composed

Class composition analysis sees class not as a thing, not as something given or pre-existent, but rather as something that happens. Class gets composed, decomposed and recomposed on a continual basis. A compositional analysis works by abstracting the two dynamics that drive the composition of class. Firstly, class is composed by the specific ways in which capital's need for self-expansion structures and constrains our lives. Capitalism produces a world in which our own needs and desires get subordinated beneath the drive to add another zero to an accounting spreadsheet. Just as a shark must keep moving to breathe and live, capital needs to grow, by around 3 per cent a year, or the whole system starts to break down.[30] But this is only half the story of class. The common experience of the various ways capital structures and cramps our lives forms the basis of our attempts to overcome those constraints – to be more than just workers, renters, debtors and housewives. This second dynamic is understood in the tradition as the drive for working-class autonomy from capital.[31] Class composition analysis came together in the 1960s as part of an Italian Marxist intellectual movement known as *operaismo* (workerism). It was developed precisely to address a moment of intergenerational incommunicability on the Left in which the established Italian Left were unable to understand the struggles, problems and perspective of a new generation of workers.

The first indications of this generation gap came with a series of wildcat strikes in the early 1960s in Italian factories, which revealed an increasingly antagonistic attitude among younger workers not only to management but also to their own union officials. This tendency came to a head during an important strike at Fiat in 1962. The UIL union, which was politically close to the Italian Socialist Party, negotiated a return to work without consulting the strikers and independently of the other unions involved. In response hundreds of angry workers surrounded the union's offices in Piazza Statuto, Turin. The police were called to protect the union building and riots broke out which lasted for three days. The incident became known as 'La Rivolta di Piazza Statuto' (the Piazza Statuto revolt) and caused a huge rift on the Left.

On one side intellectuals linked to the Socialist and Communist Parties dismissed the riots as the work of provocateurs and saboteurs. But on the other side a small group of dissident Marxist sociologists linked to the political journal *Quaderni Rossi* saw the Piazza Statuto revolt as a symptom of a new style of Left politics, or as an emerging political composition. The *operaisti* identified a link between this new political outlook and the new experience of work, which they'd been detecting in a series of workers' inquiries they'd been conducting in Italian factories from the late 1950s. The inquiries revealed that a significant section of workers, often younger and often from Southern Italy, had a very different relationship to the work process than that reflected in the orthodox leftism of the time.

The Italian Communist Party was generally sympathetic to the introduction of new technology and techniques of 'scientific management', which they saw as containing a rationality that was inherently progressive beyond its usefulness for capital.[32] In the factories most union positions were held by an older generation of militants who tended to occupy more specialist technical jobs, which gave them a level of autonomy over their work process and a level of protection from being replaced. The younger workers, on the other hand, tended to occupy the less skilled positions. They had a more alienated relationship to their work and experienced the introduction of new technology and 'Taylorism' as the bosses' weapons in the battle for control over work.[33] It was this mismatch between the Left's ideological positions and the young workers' experience that produced the hostility towards their own representatives. The generational tensions were a result of the changing composition of work and workers within the factories. The *operaisti* would title this emerging class composition the mass workers.

We can understand Mario Tronti's famous Copernican inversion in this light. Tronti, an Italian philosopher who was one of the founders of *operaismo*, says that for too long we have adopted the perspective of capitalist development. We must turn this upside down and adopt the working-class point of view, the perspective of the working class as it struggles for autonomy from determination by capital.[34] Seen in its historical context this represents a critique of the Italian Communist Party, which, attached to a class composition that was passing, had taken on the perspective of capitalist development. We need to note, however, the key role that the event of the Piazza Statuto revolt played in detecting the emerging political composition of the mass workers. In fact, a later *operaista* organization, Potere Operaio, went on to claim that 'Piazza Statuto was our founding congress'.

The key analytical distinction in class composition analysis is between the technical and political composition of the class. It's useful to look at how this analysis arose in the work of Sergio Bologna.[35] Bologna was a historian attached to *operaismo* and it was his attempt to understand the recurrence of certain forms of events that led him to develop the categories of technical and political composition. Bologna wanted to explain why working-class struggle seemed to move in a wave-like pattern, with very similar forms of struggle and organization emerging suddenly across many different countries and contexts. In particular, he wanted to understand the wave of workers' councils that had sprung up across Germany in 1918–19 and swept across Italy in what became known as the Two Red Years (the 'Biennio Rosso') of 1919–20. The latter culminated in a huge wave of factory occupations in Milan and Turin, some of which restarted production under workers' control. Bologna was drawn to this period because the Italian Communist Party (CPI) had emerged out of its wake. Workers' councils were the political form that could reveal a common technical composition beneath the later ideology of the CPI.

There is, of course, an element of imitation and inspiration involved in the circulation of struggles, but, Bologna argued, this is facilitated by the dynamics of capitalism. As new technology and reorganizations of the work process are spread across different contexts by capitalist competition, a similar experience of work and life are spread with them. It's this technical base, and the culture of work through which workers conformed to it, that makes up the technical composition of the class. Indeed, when talking about the technical composition of the class we should really think in terms of a techno-economic paradigm, including not just technologies but also the dominant business models they are entwined with and the government policies that facilitate them. Each technical composition has certain affordances which influence the shape of struggle. They make some forms of struggle more difficult and therefore less likely to occur and be effective. But the struggle for working-class autonomy cannot be suppressed forever, and when it re-emerges it will bear the form of the technical composition's affordances. Bologna's analysis of the German council movement revealed the militants as what he called 'professional workers', or what we might call craft workers, with a high degree of autonomy over, and knowledge of, the work process. This facilitated a councilist form of politics in which revolution is imagined as a matter of occupying the factories and restarting production under workers' control. The Fordist reorganization of the work process and the Taylorist forms of management that accompanied it were specifically designed to take that knowledge away from the workers and place it in the hands of the managers.[36] In reflection of this the political composition of the mass workers tended to express workers' autonomy through the refusal of work. They aimed to do less work to exercise autonomy outside of it rather than identifying with work and wanting to take it over.

Generational dynamics come into the analysis because each one of these cycles, each moment of political recomposition, requires transformations in ways of acting, organizing and thinking in which generational lag plays a role. There's a longstanding tendency for the Left to mistake a specific political composition for a universal model of politics. Detecting the connection between the technical composition and political composition of the class becomes much more difficult to determine as we move into post-Fordist forms of production, in which the experience of work becomes much more variegated and the mass workplaces get broken up and distributed across networks; as finance becomes hegemonic and the extraction of rent more central to capital; and as neoliberal forms of governance obscure and deny class antagonism. Under these conditions thinking in terms of political generations and events can be a useful way of understanding emerging political composition. In an incredibly complex and variable technical composition it's hard to work out what elements have political valency. Events can help indicate this. It quite often takes a political event or explosion to indicate that a new political composition is in formation.

In the next chapter we examine the impact of the event of 2008 on the technical composition of the working class. I will argue that the older generation are still tied to the neoliberal hegemony of finance while the young seek to escape it. The event of 2008 provides a shared generational location for the young and disadvantaged. But the emergence of a coherent new political generation requires events of a different kind. A Left generation requires a rupture caused by a moment of collective action that exceeds the existing sense of social and political possibility. In chapter 3 we will name these types of events 'moments of excess' and propose the 2011 international wave of protests and revolutions as a prime example. We will examine this wave as the first iteration of an emerging political composition, examining its forms for traces of 2008's impacts on the technical composition. The events of 2011 created a Left generational unit, and in chapter 4 we examine this unit's turn to electoral politics to gain hegemony over the much larger but politically ambiguous generation of 2008. This turn brought them into conflict with a previous Left generation, the Third Way Left, formed by the events of 1989 and characterized by their compromise with neoliberalism. The event of 2008 undermined that generation's formative assumptions, leaving them unable to understand or deal with the current generation gap. This means it falls to Generation Left to deal with the current situation, and in chapter 5 I suggest ways that the current generation gap can be overcome. This will involve reinventing the categories of youth and adulthood to break their current entanglement with private property ownership, shifting them instead towards the kinds of common ownership which can act as a solution to the generational divide over access to material security. Only in this way can we ensure that our current 'storms of youth precede brilliant days' for all generations.[37]

2

Generation Left (Behind)

Generations are caused by events, or, put more accurately, events set the conditions from which distinct political generations can emerge. That must mean that events leave marks on the resulting generations. If we can understand the compositional effects of the event of 2008, then we can identify, in subsequent chapters, the scars it has left on the politics that are emerging. It seems straightforward to say that the financial crisis of 2008 is the generational event of our time, but what sort of event was it and what were its effects? This isn't easy to answer because the meaning of an event, and, indeed, whether something counts as a significant event at all, is not determined at the time. It depends on what happens afterwards, how it goes down in history. In that regard 2008 has had a complicated and contested afterlife.

Generation Left (Behind)

2008 Did Not Take Place

Events always contain a moment after which things aren't the same again. In 2008 that moment came with the bankruptcy of Lehman Brothers investment bank on 15 September. The next day this caused the insolvency of AIG, the largest insurance company in the world. The resulting cascade of uncertainty over the solvency of other financial institutions caused interbank lending to seize up and the cost of borrowing to rocket. It was this that spread the crisis to the 'real' economy, causing global production to shrink by 13 per cent and global trade to reduce by 20 per cent.[1] From the autobiographies of Ben Bernanke, the Chair of the US Federal Reserve, and Alistair Darling, the UK Chancellor of the Exchequer, we now know that by October 2008 the ATMs came within hours of closing.[2] Only massive intervention from the State prevented the complete collapse of the financial sector.

The day after AIG declared bankruptcy, Bernanke and US Treasury Secretary Hank Paulson went to Congress with a three-page bill. It amounted to a $750 billion blank cheque, which they could spend without review 'by any court of law or any administrative agency'. Congress had been promised that $700 billion of mortgages would be bought to enable modification in favour of mortgage holders. A key section of the bill authorized the Treasury Secretary to 'facilitate loan modifications to prevent avoidable foreclosures'. He quickly changed his mind. Not only were existing debt obligations enforced, but the money was, in effect, given straight to the banks to prop up their balance sheets.[3] The direction set then is ongoing still. States have taken on the bad debts of the financial sector, providing them with favourable loans and, through quantitative easing programmes, huge amounts of free money. The bailouts are one of the greatest non-wartime mobilizations of resources in human history. Their sole aim was preventing a technical financial event from turning into a political event, a political turning point. This allowed reform of the financial sector to be limited and neoliberal ideology to escape reassessment.

One of the most peculiar aspects of the last decade was the disappearance of the 2008 financial crisis. In the immediate aftermath of the Lehman collapse discussion focused on the causes of the crisis and the measures needed to prevent its re-occurrence. 'Free market' ideology came under serious pressure. Former Federal Reserve Chairman Alan Greenspan famously told Congress he had found a flaw in his thinking, and systemic reform of the financial sector seemed inevitable. Yet within six months the event of 2008 had disappeared behind the spectre of deficits in government budgets. These deficits, in which a country's expenses exceed its revenue, were primarily caused by the reduced tax take from a shrinking economy and increased spending to pay for the bailouts. Yet these effects of the financial crisis were suddenly treated as though they were its cause.[4] By 2010 austerity had become enshrined as the primary policy response and talk of reforming finance was sidelined. Instead the financial sector was lavished with an ocean of free money paid for by public spending cuts and wage restraints.

In this way a technical crisis in a sector of capital was turned into a moment of decomposition for the working class. It would be farcical to blame the financial crisis on Muslims, immigrants or the unemployed, but once that event was out of view resentments could breed over access to a shrinking pot of resources. The event of 2008 changed the technical composition of society, new class fractures opened up and points of non-communication solidified as immediate interests diverged. The real story of the past decade has been an acceleration in the obscene concentration of wealth. In 2018 82 per cent of new global wealth went to the top 1 per cent,[5] while in 2017 Oxfam reported that just eight men owned the same amount of wealth as the bottom 50 per cent of the global population, 3.7 billion individuals.[6] The bailouts and the post-crisis economy might well entail the biggest transfer of wealth to a tiny elite in human history. It has taken a concerted political effort to stop this fact being the central political issue of our time. But that effort is facilitated by the rarefied lives of the global elite. They simply don't figure in our day-to-day existence. Political divisions arise, therefore, through proxy effects on the general population.

The post-crisis world economy has become addicted to quantitative easing and low interest rates. It is proving near impossible to remove these supports without causing the whole edifice to collapse. This produces an economy in which saving is disincentivized, financial markets are awash with cash but demand for business investment is tepid – the perfect environment for asset price bubbles. Stock markets have quickly recovered to record highs, while property prices have remained high in most countries. As older generations are more likely to own assets, usually property, then intergenerational injustice has become supercharged. The young, on the other hand, are dependent on wages, which have been flat in the US while in the UK the

2010s will be 'the weakest decade for pay growth since the Napoleonic wars'.[7]

Many of the trends towards intergenerational injustice go back several decades, but the emergence of age as a significant political divide has only taken off in the last few years.[8] The acceleration in injustice helps explain the timing but it doesn't fully explain why what was previously tolerable has suddenly became intolerable. Neoliberalism is not just a way of ordering the economy; it is also a model for governing our lives that constricts what appears socially and politically possible. This dramatically alters how changes in material circumstances play out politically. Actually existing neoliberalism has been through several changes during the 40 years of its existence. It has therefore interacted differently with different generations. Any assessment of the generational impact of 2008 must take this into account.

Periodizing Neoliberalism

In a 2016 article called 'The New Neoliberalism' Will Davies usefully divides the history of actually existing neoliberalism into three distinct periods based on the motivating ethic holding it together at that time.[9] The years 1979–89, he argues, were dominated by a combative ethic, while the years 1989–2008 saw attempts to re-orient around a normative ethic. I disagree with his characterization of the third period, post-2008, as punitive, but the periodization is still useful. It helps reveal how neoliberal logics and practices developed in one context survive, in reworked form, in subsequent ones. In a world in which many neoliberal practices no longer make sense this helps explain their persistence. Yet if we're to understand the compositional effects of 2008, we need more than an understanding of neoliberalism's internal logic. We also need to reverse our perspective and grasp neoliberalism from the point of view of working-class autonomy. What political composition did neoliberalism set out to decompose, and what potential recomposition is it trying to ward off now?

Davies argues that during its combative stage neoliberalism was held together by its mission to defeat socialism. He dates this period from 1979, the year of Margaret Thatcher's election, but neoliberalism was established as an intellectual and political project well before this.[10] Davies locates the birth of neoliberalism as a distinctive project in Ludwig von Mises' 1922 contribution to the Socialist Calculation debate. The absolutist, combative style of neoliberal

39

critique was established by Mises' argument that the only rational way to organize society is to use price signals to coordinate activity through market structures. Dismissing all other modes of thought as irrational creates an intellectual isolationism that helps explain the post-2008 inability of neoliberalism to reform itself.

For Mark Fisher one result of neoliberalism's combative drive is what he calls capitalist realism, where the only conceivable reality is one dominated by ever-intensifying capitalist social relations.[11] Yet in the last few years before his tragic and untimely death Fisher had increasingly adopted a reversal of perspective, understanding capitalism as a machine for warding off the recurring, though often fugitive, potential for a society of common wealth and non-domination. He became interested, in particular, in the social and political potential of the 1970s that neoliberalism prevented. The Left was undergoing its own generational battle in the run-up to the neoliberal era. The official Left of the time was set on protecting the gains the working class received in a post-war settlement between capital and labour, which linked rising wages to rising productivity as a means of maintaining profitability. In the UK this deal was explicit. The head of the employers and the leader of the unions would meet at the Prime

Minister's house to hammer out a deal over 'beer and sandwiches'. As part of this settlement the State became the guarantor of the population's social reproduction through state pensions, unemployment insurance and, in most countries, health care free at the point of delivery. This deal went into crisis in the 1970s owing in part to attempts by young workers and Left movements to push beyond its limits and constraints.

The key social movements of the time, second-wave feminism, gay liberation and the anti-racist and anti-colonial movements, were revolts by those sectors that got dealt a bad hand in the post-war deal. As an accompaniment, the youth movement, the counterculture and the rising militancy of young workers can be seen as attempts to exceed the deal while rejecting the boredom and conformity of the 'Fordist' world that went with it. The unprecedented material security that post-war social democracy gave to working-class youth bred rising confidence and assertiveness. The young Left increasingly saw the post-war deal as a staging post on the road to more democratic and participative forms of socialism.[12] Full employment, high wages and a safety net provided by the State allowed new sectors of society the time and space to explore what freedom meant from their perspective. The results are visible in cultural production. The 1970s and 1980s are still regarded as the highpoint of pop cultural innovation and experimentation. As working- and middle-class youth exercised unprecedented control over the direction of culture, they pioneered new ways of living and began to produce desires that could not be met under Fordist capitalism, or perhaps under capitalism of any sort. A generation gap opened on the Left between those wishing to recompose Left politics around these new desires and an older Left who feared the disintegration of the discipline needed to maintain their post-war gains.[13]

For capital the crises of the 1970s manifested as inflationary spirals that undermined profitability. Sections of capital found neoliberal theories attractive because they had a story to explain the situation. Inflation was high, they argued, because wages and social spending were too high. There was too much money in the system chasing too few goods and services. The problem was, as Samuel Huntington and his colleagues famously put it, 'an excess of democracy'.[14] Wages were rising owing to workers' increased willingness and ability to assert their interests through industrial struggle. Social spending was increasing because previously unorganized segments of society were able to exert democratic pressure on elected politicians. More

than this, sections of the Left were producing proposals for democratic control in workplaces and the
extension of more participatory forms of democracy across society.[15] In some ways the neoliberal
analysis was right. The crisis of the 1970s produced
a decision point. We could either pursue a radical
extension of democracy that pushed beyond the
constraints of capital or start a radical rollback of
democracy to reassert capitalist control. It's for this
reason that Mark Fisher argues:

> [N]eoliberalism's real target was not its official
> enemies – the decadent monolith of the Soviet bloc,
> and the crumbling compacts of social democracy
> and the New Deal, which were collapsing under the
> weight of their own contradictions. Instead, neo-
> liberalism is best understood as a project aimed at
> destroying – to the point of making them unthinkable
> – the experiments in democratic socialism and liber-
> tarian communism that were efflorescing at the end
> of the 60s and the beginning of the 70s.[16]

In his work towards an unfinished book called
Acid Communism Fisher began using the prism of
consciousness inflation to reinterpret the practices
of the 1970s Left. The concept comes from the
consciousness-raising groups that were the organizational bedrock of the 1970s feminist movement.
These were small groups of women who met

regularly to discuss their lives and link their problems to structural causes.[17] Alongside this example Fisher examined the heightened class consciousness of the period as well as the consciousness-expanding impact of psychedelic culture on the youth movement. Consciousness raising, then, encompasses a series of functions. It involves identifying the structural causes of the social constraints that are placed on your life. It includes the increased confidence and capacity that comes with seeing yourself as part of a powerful collective actor rather than an isolated individual. And it also includes that expansion of social and political possibility that comes when what is presented as necessary and inevitable is revealed as merely contingent and therefore, in principle, changeable. As a corollary to this Fisher began to conceive of neoliberalism as a project of consciousness deflation. Positioning this analysis within the combative phase of neoliberalism helps explain why attacks on the material security and institutions of the working class took precedence over all other concerns.

The initial neoliberal route to consciousness deflation lay through economic deflation. The dramatic rises in interest rates in the late 1970s and early 1980s brought inflation under control but only by provoking a recession. The resulting unemployment disciplined workers and pinned back their hopes and expectations. A combination of militarized policing and legal and financial strangulation then defeated the union movement. In the UK real wages have stagnated since this point; in the US they have declined. It was only later, as the recession lifted, that financial inducements were added to the consciousness deflation armoury. Rising house prices were the main tool for this seduction as the sale of public housing and the deregulation of finance began the financialization of everyday life. Combative neoliberalism placed violent impediments in the path of a viable Left future and provided financial inducements towards individualized (or family-based) models of the neoliberal good life.

In the generational blame game genre there are a set of conservative narratives that blame the current state of crisis not on the Millennials but on the Baby Boomers. Books such as *A Generation of Sociopaths* by Bruce Gibney[18] and films such as *Generation Zero* by Steve Bannon present a story that rolls seamlessly from the perceived self-indulgence of the counterculture to the greedy selfishness of the early 2000s. They suggest familiar causes for this generational flaw: lax parenting and the affordances of then dominant media technologies; Boomers were after all the first generation native to TV.

Seeing neoliberalism as consciousness deflation suggests a different story. The Baby Boomers are a defeated generation. The Left generational project that looked so strong in the 1960s and 1970s was defeated in the 1980s and 1990s. Accusations of sociopathic selfishness elide that defeat and treat its symptoms as a cause.

Neoliberal Common Sense (Consciousness Razing)

Neoliberalism's second stage began with the 'Fall of the Berlin Wall' in 1989. It's a phrase that stands in for a wider process of global realignment as the Soviet bloc countries underwent a sudden and harsh transition to a neoliberal version of capitalism. Around the same time the Chinese Communist Party suppressed the Tiananmen Square rebellion and opened up parts of its economy to foreign investment. Taken together, these had two profound effects. Firstly, the disappearance of an economic bloc that was, at least in some sense, non-capitalist had a dramatic impact on dominant political imaginaries. 'There is No Alternative' came to seem a statement of fact. Secondly, over just a couple of years the global labour force available for exploitation by a newly mobile capital doubled in size.[19]

This unprecedented event significantly reduced the bargaining power of labour. As workers around the world were less able to assert their interests, hopes for improving life through socialist means were severely curtailed. Social democratic parties around the world accepted some form of neoliberalism as the horizon of political possibility.

'What is neoliberalism in the absence of socialism – what provides its orientation or ethical coherence?'[20] Will Davies answers his own question by suggesting that neoliberalism moves from its destructive emphasis to become a constructive project based on a normative ethic. This period saw the extension of (pseudo-)competitive market relations into more areas of life. The process was given a normative sheen by using competitiveness as the measure of 'fairness'. 'The task of government was now to ensure that "winners" were clearly distinguishable from "losers", and that the contest was perceived as fair.'[21] This normative ethic deflated consciousness by limiting what seemed politically and socially possible but it also occupied the space of the Left. It was the 'Third Way' centre Left that drank most deeply of the neoliberal Kool-Aid and became its fiercest advocates. They shifted neoliberalism away from the social conservatism of its combative era towards those elements of the feminist, anti-racist and gay liberation movements which could be aligned with consumerism and competitive labour markets.

Mark Fisher captures the prevailing attitude as 'a pragmatic adjustment'. 'Capitalist realism', he goes on to say, 'isn't the direct endorsement of neoliberal doctrine; it's the idea that, whether we like it or not, the world is governed by neoliberal ideas, and that won't change. There's no point fighting the inevitable.'[22] To understand how competitive markets construct this sense of inevitability we can look at the format of reality TV, the key cultural genre of the 2000s. Early reality shows produced a constructed 'realism' that leant heavily on the tradition of documentary. The usual format brought a group of strangers together in an unusual environment; the results were then filmed and edited into a dramatic narrative. In the early 2000s the genre was reinvented, with shows such as *Big Brother* and *The Apprentice* formed around the principle of competition. A competitive 'voting out' element was added in order to stimulate anti-social, backstabbing, competitive behaviour. Producers continually tweak the formats to ensure this behaviour dominates. As contestants grasp the institutional logic of the situation, they alter their behaviour to conform to these expectations.[23]

Neoliberal institutional reforms, and the managerial practices that accompany them, follow a similar model. Neoliberalism is different from classical liberalism, and indeed other iterations of capitalism, owing to its drive to re-found the whole of society around an ethos of competition. Neoliberal theorists recognize that competitive markets are not 'naturally' occurring. They must be constructed by an active, interventionist State.[24] Extending them beyond the 'economic' sphere requires dramatic institutional reform and intrusive management practices to assess behaviour. When we interact with competitive market structures we must conform to their logic or we will lose out. Our forced engagement with these 'markets' acts as a kind of training. It trains us to adopt a particular subjectivity, a particular mode of thinking and acting. The institutions we interact with on a daily basis are continually tweaked to ensure they reward ruthlessly competitive, selfish and self-promoting behaviour while penalizing those who behave in other ways. Through repetition we internalize this institutional logic, come to anticipate it and act accordingly. It eventually becomes the common-sense view of what human beings are 'really' like.[25] This is consciousness deflation writ large. The complex potential of humanity becomes reduced to a single model of life, but it's a model we can't live in. The epidemics of depression, insomnia and mental distress are testament to that. What a lot of planning, effort and resources it's taken to put that feeling of anxiety into your stomach.

The Persistence of the Zombie

So what's changed since 2008? For Will Davies neoliberalism has taken a turn towards the punitive. He argues, for instance, that the morality tied up with debt has predisposed us to accept austerity as punishment for unearned debt-fuelled growth. There is something to this, but I think it's more useful to understand neoliberalism as entering its zombie stage: it is 'dead yet still dominant'.[26] The key characteristic of zombies is brain death. Their bodies keep operating but without conscious thought. Zombies can only act habitually, pursuing a monomaniacal hunger to consume the living even though their bodies gain no benefit. The zombie is a body stripped of its ability to alter course and decide on a different future. Zombies represent violent stasis. They don't change, they don't adapt, they just persist. Similarly, the distinguishing characteristic of post-crisis neoliberalism is its inability to reform itself, despite a decade-long stagnation. Neoliberalism has stopped making sense, even on its own terms, yet the project hasn't stopped. Neoliberal ideology has lost its coherence, yet its policies roll out unabated. This makes the situation strange and contradictory. We're placed in an ideological double bind. We are still trained to adopt a neoliberal world-view by the institutional logic of the organizations we engage with and the debt-based relations within which we are trapped, but for most it's impossible to believe this will lead to a better life. The organs of the neoliberal body keep churning out neoliberal subjects, but we are now robbed of the teleology that would make sense of our suffering. Zombie neoliberalism doesn't offer us anything; it just persists.

The debt-based financialization of everyday life is structured by Gary Becker's concept of *human capital*. Debt encourages us to adopt the perspective of capital. We are encouraged to interpret our activity as investments in ourselves that must be judged on the metrics of a return on investment. It produces a subjectivity which, as Wendy Brown nicely summarizes,

> is concerned with enhancing its portfolio values in all domains of its life, an activity undertaken

through practices of self-investment and attracting investors. Whether through social media 'followers', 'likes' and 'retweets', through rankings and ratings for every activity and domain, or through more directly monetized practices, the pursuit of education, training, leisure, reproduction, consumption, and more are increasingly configured as strategic decisions and practices related to enhancing the self's future value.[27]

For older generations, who are more likely to own property, the human capital metaphor might still make sense. But for younger cohorts the collapse in prospects has made further self-investment irrational. Over the last decade, for instance, the returns on education have lowered dramatically. The chances that graduates will get graduate-level jobs have massively reduced, so why haven't student numbers dropped? In times of stagnation the human capital metaphor breaks down, but without alternative modes of living we are still forced to engage with institutions based on its logic. As Maurizio Lazzarato writes:

> The current crisis stems from the fact that . . . this subjective figure has failed . . . the promise that 'work on the self' was supposed to offer 'labor' in terms of emancipation (pleasure, a sense of accomplishment, recognition, experimentation with new

forms of life, upward mobility, etc.) has been trans-
formed into the imperative to take upon oneself the
risks and costs for which neither business nor the
State are willing to pay. . . . In the current crisis, for
the majority of the population 'work on the self'
means no more than the 'entrepreneurial' management of unemployment, debt, wage and revenue
cuts, reductions in social services and rising taxes.[28]

The intrusive evaluation linked to debt and managerialism was once attached to a story of aspiration;
now it is felt as an imposition without consent, a
constraint on freedom. For the young in particular
there are few financial inducements to align their
hopes with finance capital. Debt requires a subject
who can keep a promise into the future.[29] It requires
a zombie subject who can't change direction or
risk a rupture with their present selves. That's why
student debt is so pernicious and onerous. The
responsibilities of future adulthood are imposed
upon the young before they have a chance to set
their own goals. It robs young people of their youth,
of their chance to reinvent themselves.

When the common sense of a society stops
making sense but change through collective action
seems out of reach, people must create ad hoc subjectivities from the material to hand. One solution
for the more affluent young is to double down on

'self-investment' in the hope that it will pay off. The accusations of narcissism levelled at Millennials should be seen in this light. Young people with fewer resources, on the other hand, must find narratives that make sense of their 'entrepreneurial management' of debt, low wages and precarious work.

We can see evidence of this in the work of Jennifer Silva. Her interviews with 100 young working-class Americans found a subjectivity 'characterized by low expectations of work, wariness towards romantic commitment, widespread distrust of social institutions, profound isolation from others, and an overriding focus on their emotions and psychic health'.[30] The dominant narrative through which these youths understand their lives is a therapeutic one which works as follows:

> first, it compels one to identify pathological thoughts and behaviors; second, to locate the hidden source of these pathologies within one's past; third, to give voice to one's story of suffering in communication with others; and finally, to triumph over one's past by bringing into being an emancipated and independent self.[31]

It's a narrative structure that produces a 'sense of forward-moving progress',[32] but it has severe political limitations. Silva compares it unfavourably to 'social movements like feminism' in which

> self-awareness, or naming one's problems, was the first step to radical collective awareness. For this generation, it is the only step, completely detached from any kind of solidarity; while they struggle with similar, and structurally rooted, problems, there is no sense of 'we'. . . . [W]ithout a collective sense of structural inequalities, the suffering and betrayal born of de-industrialization, inequality, and risk is interpreted as individual failure.[33]

2008 Eventually Took Place

The bailouts were an attempt to displace the event of 2008 temporally by kicking its economic impacts further down the road. Austerity was an attempt to displace the event of 2008 politically by obscuring who was to blame. The result was a slow-motion crisis in which age came to be a key point of fracture. At first this was hard to see as active consent turned into passive consent and then fell into resentment. Generational inequalities which were previously tolerable suddenly became intolerable. The combined but uneven collapse of neoliberal aspiration has led to a crisis in the way young people make sense of the world. As a result, the nascent generation of 2008 is large and disgruntled but it is also politically ambiguous. The crisis of neoliberalism has not been resolved. The direction this generation takes will decide how that crisis ends.

3

Generation Explosion

The crisis of 2008 was an event of a certain kind. We might call it a passive event because it appeared as something that happened to us. It feels like it's been caused by forces beyond our control, akin to an act of nature. Events such as this tend to produce the feeling that possibility is closing down. The sense of possibility attached to one social form goes into crisis but new possibilities have yet to cohere. Events of a certain magnitude, even if they are passively received, can produce the divergence of experiences from which generational differences emerge. They create, we could say, the raw material for generational emergence, but they don't automatically create a coherent generational outlook. The event of 2008 produced the potential for a large but politically ambiguous generation. Mannheim would call the common experience of this group a shared 'generational location', but that is not the same as a coherent political generation, which requires 'similarly "located" contemporaries [to] participate in a common destiny and in the ideas and concepts which are in some way bound up with its unfolding'.[1] Those initiating that process form 'generational units' among those who share 'a certain affinity in the way in which all move with and are formed by their common experiences'.[2]

Mannheim is clear that generations can overlap with conservative, liberal or socialist movements, but I would supplement his theory by distinguishing between political generations of the Right and the Left. It is difficult for Left generational units to form around passive events because they need possibility to open up so new groups can participate in self-rule. By contrast, Corey Robin defines conservatism as 'a meditation on – and theoretical rendition of – the felt experience of having power, seeing it threatened, and trying to win it back'.[3] The closing down of existing possibility associated with passive events can produce this kind of feeling and allow right-wing narratives to take hold. Left generational units are better suited to what we might call 'active' events. These are events which their participants experience as something that they have actively constructed with others. This tends to cause an expansion of social and political possibility. It is worth thinking a little more about that experience in order to see the influence it has on emerging Left generations.

Moments of Excess

Aristide Zolberg provides a useful sketch of such events in his seminal article 'Moments of Madness'. In the introductory passage he outlines the challenge they pose to political thinking:

> If politics is 'the art of the possible,' what are we to make of moments when human beings living in modern societies believe that 'all is possible'? We know with assurance that such moments occur, if only because those who experience them are acutely conscious of their unusual state. Speaking with tongues, they urgently record their most intimate feelings. Furthermore, they are often aware of affinities across time and space with others in similar circumstances.[4]

Zolberg draws on this urgent record and compares testimony from six Parisian events, beginning with the revolt of 1848. The article, written in 1972, is undoubtedly a response to the Paris *événements* of 1968, and taking his cue from the awareness he found there 'of affinities across time and space with others in similar circumstances', he seeks out what is common in the experience of these moments. In 1968 there were living links to the 1936 wave of factory occupations that accompanied the Popular Front government, as well as to the contagious enthusiasm that followed the 1944 Liberation of Paris. Contemporary commentators on May '68 also raised the antecedents of the revolutions of 1848 and the Paris Commune of 1871. Zolberg treats the commonality of experience he finds in these Parisian events as an example of a wider phenomenon, and indeed testimony from them is quite consistent.

> The recurrence of these moments over one hundred and twenty years, recognizably the same in spite of variations, gives the phenomenon a persuasive concreteness each event may not possess individually. ... Whatever the attitudes of the writers at the time of writing, they record intense moments of festive joy. ... Minds and bodies are liberated; human beings feel that they are in direct touch with one another as well as with their inner selves. ... Simultaneously, there is a disposition to encounter the *déjà vu*; through the medium of collective memories recorded in sophisticated or demotic culture, in historical works or in folklore, human

beings connect the moment with others. Liberated
from the constraints of time and place, and circumstances, from history, men choose their parts from
the available repertory or forge new ones in an act
of creation. Dreams become possibilities.[5]

There is a tendency within political science and
theory either to dismiss such moments as epiphe-
nomenal, or, in the case of the French and American
Revolutions, to treat them as foundational but
exceptional. As Zolberg says: 'Since we cannot
ignore them, we segregate them from our main con-
cern, the universe of normal political events.'[6] The
opposing, though related, tendency is to treat the
experiences found in such events as in some ways
'more real' than those of 'ordinary life' and to treat
the political forms through which that experience is
expressed as the model for a universal politics to be
applied in any situation. Instead I want to focus on
how such moments are conditioned by the contexts
from which they emerge even though they exceed
them. Doing so will allow us to use these moments
to better understand the political possibilities and
limitations of the present. From this we can gain
a clearer sense of how such moments can fit into
ongoing projects of political change.

We saw in the previous chapter how the logic
of the institutions we interact with can create a

constrained sense of social and political possibility. It's a contraction of horizons that's reinforced by the technical and media environments within which we live our habitual lives. As Maurizio Lazzarato puts it, 'Those who govern have the power to define problems and formulate questions (which they term "the possibilities") and establish in this way what is noteworthy, important, relevant, feasible, worth acting on and speaking about.'[7] The type of event with which we're concerned may produce the sensation that 'all is possible', but possibility is constrained in different ways in different historical and social contexts. What is being witnessed is the opening up of possibility, or more specifically the exceeding of a particular constriction of possibility. It's for this reason that I want to call these events 'moments of excess'.[8] Each individual event of this kind contains its own moment of excess: the point at which what was previously tolerated suddenly becomes intolerable. Sometimes it's an individual action that produces this moment: the self-immolation of Mohamed Bouazizi, for example, which sparked the Tunisian revolution in December 2010. Sometimes it's a collective action, such as an unexpectedly large or militant demonstration. The storming and occupation of 30 Millbank, the Conservative Party offices in London, in November

2010 is an example of this. It sparked two months of student protests and university occupations. Either way, the moments of excess do not emerge from nowhere. They are rather crystallizations of longer-term trends and changes in class composition, which put pre-existing subjectivities under pressure. The explosion of possibility experienced in a moment of excess exceeds the subjectivities with which we have lived our everyday lives. But there is no such thing as a completely fresh contact with a moment of excess. The narratives through which we make sense of the world leave a trace in the moments in which we exceed them.

Recognizing this allows us to incorporate such moments into a class composition analysis. As we saw with our discussion of the Piazza Statuto revolt, moments of excess have been key indicators of a changing class composition. To be more specific, by crystallizing the emergence of new attitudes and new political problems, these events play a key role in the emergence and recognition of new political compositions. They involve, as Zolberg points out, 'a sort of intensive learning experience whereby new ideas, formulated initially in coteries, sects, etc., emerge as widely held beliefs among much larger publics'.[9] By crystallizing and framing a problem, they force observers to make a decision on whether to align themselves with the old or the new space of possibility. It's this process that produces what autonomists call the circulation of struggles, in which similar organizational forms and repertoires of action emerge simultaneously across many different contexts and where people recognize themselves in the actions of others. As the Italian writing collective Wu Ming put it when discussing a wave of mutinies by Italian soldiers on hearing about the Russian Revolution, '[T]hose proletarians asked themselves: "What does this remote event look like? What does it *feel* like?" And they answered: "It feels like what I'd like to do myself!"'[10] As events in individual cities or countries spread in a wave-like fashion, they enter into a relationship of mutual amplification, producing a moment of excess on an international scale. It is these moments that can prove to be generational.

In times such as ours in which the technical composition of society is so complex and variegated, the common shape of events emerging in a wave across many different countries can provide strong clues as to what is common across these apparently different contexts. The shape taken by a moment of excess, the problems it forms around, the organizational and action repertoires that it produces, all indicate the politically salient elements of a changing composition. They show the direction the new generation of politics is moving in. But it would be a mistake to accept these moments on their own terms. The resonances between them come from a certain similarity, or compatibility, in technical compositions. And as such they will bear the scars of the pre-existing experiences and subjectivities of their participants.[11] We can think of moments of excess as the first draft of a potential new politics, but political composition is also a political project in which militants, or a generational unit, can attempt to innovate new forms of organization and modes of struggle in order to overcome the limits, blockages and moments of non-communication inherited from the underlying technical composition. Although it appears that these moments all produce similar affects, the forms through which those affects are expressed and received reflect the conjuncture from which they originate. By tracing these forms, and the functions they fulfil, back to the technical composition from which they emerge, we can better understand how the same style of politics may take new forms in the future. However, the scars of existing society are not the only inheritances we have to think through. Any new generation of politics also has to position itself among, and interact with, the ideas and practices of already existing, and past, Left generations. There are generational dynamics to how that plays out.

First Time as Tragedy . . .

One of the resources we can draw on to conceptualize this problem is Marx's great text on historical repetitions, 'The Eighteenth Brumaire of Louis Bonaparte':

> Human beings make their own history, but they do not make it just as they please; they do not make it under circumstances directly encountered, given and transmitted from the past. The tradition of all the dead generations weighs like a nightmare upon the brains of the living. And just when they seem engaged in revolutionising themselves and things, in creating something that has never yet existed, precisely in such periods of revolutionary crisis they anxiously borrow from them names, battle cries and costumes in order to present the new scene of world history in their time-honoured disguise and in this borrowed language.[12]

The starting point here is that we only rarely get the chance to become historical actors. We only rarely confront the possibility of collectively breaking with the historical conditioning that limits how our lives can be lived. During these moments of excess there's an understandable tendency to draw on, and repeat, the traditions of past generations of struggle. During moments of excess people encounter experiences, problems and degrees of freedom that they've not faced previously. It makes sense in this situation for them to seek out antecedents to help orientate themselves. Failure to learn from the experience of those who have faced similar problems would leave us disorientated and unarmed in the face of historical conditioning, helpless to stop the old world reasserting itself.

There are, however, different modes in which this repetition can take place. In a famous line that precedes the passage above, Marx says, 'All facts and personages of great importance in world history occur, as it were, twice . . . the first time as tragedy, the second as farce'.[13] Reading this passage, Gilles Deleuze finds that

> historical repetition is . . . a condition of historical action itself. . . . [H]istorical actors can create only on condition that they identify themselves with figures from the past. . . . [R]epetition is comic when it falls short – that is, when instead of leading to metamorphosis and the production of something new, it forms a kind of involution, the opposite of authentic creation.[14]

When the organizational models, forms of acting and interpretive grid of a previous Left generation are simply overlaid onto the new situation, the new movement folds in on itself, obscuring the potential to address the present. We are all too familiar with the farce of treating each new movement as a simple repetition of 1917, 1936 or 1968, failing to recognize that the forms being repeated emerged from a political composition that no longer exists. If contemporary Left generations are to prevent the inheritance of past generations from weighing 'like a nightmare upon the brains of the living', then they must not repeat those traditions uncritically. A non-comic repetition is one that allows the new to emerge by recognizing its connection to current circumstances. Authentic creation requires forms of repetition that 'constantly criticize themselves, constantly interrupt themselves in their own course, return to the apparently accomplished, in order to begin anew'.[15] Now that we have established this schema we can apply it to the events that sparked Generation Left.

The Generation of 2011

If 2008 was the 'passively received' event that produced a generational location, then 2011 was the moment of excess that gave birth to an international Left generation. 2011 was a historic year of protest. *Time* magazine even gave its annual person of the year award to the generic category of 'The Protestor'. Like most iconic years it started early and finished late. I would date the start of the wave of protests, revolutions and square occupations to late 2010 and the coincidence of the UK student movement and the beginning of the Tunisian revolution. The latter sparked the Arab Spring wave of revolutions and protests in early 2011, and as these revolutions played out, the action moved back to Europe, when on 15 May a huge demonstration in Madrid turned into an occupation of Puerta del Sol square. The massive movement of protests and square occupations that then blossomed across Spain became known as the 15M or 'Indignados'. A similar movement of protest camps emerged in Greece a few weeks later before the international wave of Occupy camps was sparked in September by the establishment of the Occupy Wall Street camp in Zuccotti Park, New York.[16]

Each one of these events contained its own moment of excess in which what had previously seemed impossible suddenly burst into existence. Yet as the sequence of events unfolded and similar shapes emerged, the significance of each individual event increased. From the Arab Spring, through the Indignados, to the Occupy movement, the dominant organizational form of the 2011 protest wave was the general assembly. It gained this prominence because of its compatibility with the dominant protest repertoire, the protest camp. The camps of 2011 were semi-permanent occupations of prominent public space, often city squares. The camps facilitated other forms of protest and direct action, but it was the very fact of occupation, as a public display of dissatisfaction, which made the most impact. They acted as a pole of attraction through which the dissatisfied could congregate and find each other. Within this the general assemblies of the camps found themselves moving beyond an ancillary, supporting and merely organizational role to become central to the very purpose of the protest. The assemblies were the primary means through which people discovered and displayed their commonality. The protest camp at Tahrir Square in Cairo certainly held mass assemblies, but it was the 15M movement of the Indignados in Spain that began to introduce a particular form of consensus decision-making process. It was Occupy Wall Street, however, that did the most to spread this process and codify it as assembly practice.

Consensus decision-making has undergone continuous development within social movements for over 40 years, resulting in a highly structured process. The group Seeds for Change, who provide training in consensus decision-making, offer a useful definition: 'Consensus is a decision-making process that works creatively to include all persons making the decision. Instead of simply voting for an item and having the majority of the group getting their way, the group is committed to finding solutions that everyone can live with.'[17] The consensus process works best amongst fairly cohesive groups committed in advance to the same broad objective. The big stalling point with the consensus process is its unsuitability for making strategic decisions, that is, how to collectively generate objectives different from the ones the assembly was formed around.[18] The pressure to come to a consensus provides a bias towards the status quo. It is harder to achieve near unanimity on a proposal to break with existing practice. Veterans of the alter-globalization movement of the early 2000s introduced this consensus process into the events of 2011. At first many thought that 2011 represented a continuation of that movement, but it soon became apparent that 2008 had changed the circumstances so much that the assemblies were being used in a very different way. The assemblies of 2011 were located in busy city centres, were open to all comers and attracted a huge range of people. The aims and politics of the camps had to be built rather than assumed. As a result, when we look beyond the rhetoric we can see that the 2011 assemblies were fulfilling quite different functions to those of the alter-globalization cycle.

The Testimony Function

In 2011 emphasis was put on allowing people to express themselves, at the expense of efficient decision-making. We might call this an emphasis on testimony, and it is a good indication of the role the assemblies were really fulfilling. As Paolo Gerbaudo reports from an assembly he witnessed during the early days of the Puerta del Sol occupation, people constantly used their two minutes at the microphone to talk about the problems they had been suffering in their lives, from unemployment to bankruptcy to inadequate childcare. Each ended their testimony with the phrase '"Yo tambien soy un(a) indignado/a": "Me too – I am an indignant."'[19] In the US the same function was visible in the popular 'We are the 99 percent' website, which featured photographs of people holding pieces of cardboard upon which they'd written their stories of financial hardship.[20] The sheer aggregation of these stories and the common themes within them not only produce a sense of commonality but also stimulate a shared understanding of the structural nature of the hardship. If so many suffer from the same problems, then those problems cannot, as we might previously have felt, be due to our individual failings.

We can see in this an almost therapeutic element to the assemblies. Testifying in public about your conditions helps overcome the shame and self-blame that the techniques of consciousness deflation have inculcated in us. Yet the collective nature of this testimony produces something different to the therapeutic narrative, which Jennifer Silva's work shows is so central to how young working-class adults make sense of their lives.[21] It seems likely that the assemblies proved so attractive, at least at first, because they allowed a form of participation that was familiar to those trained by neoliberal administration. As Lazzarato puts it, 'In "individual monitoring" one is expected to come clean.'[22] Recognizing this link doesn't mean we should dismiss the assemblies as contaminated by neoliberalism. We should, rather, see it as a point of departure in our attempts to move beyond or exceed our pre-existing selves. The event of 2008 produced a crisis in the 'entrepreneurial' subjectivities so central to neo-liberalism. It's this that has opened the space for new collectivities to be built. Recognizing common problems is powerful, but tackling structural causes takes a different form of collectivity to mere aggregation. It requires collective analysis and action, and it involves us changing ourselves as we change society.

It's here that we can see another function of the general assemblies. They acted as screens upon which people could recognize themselves as newly emerging political subjects. It was often what we might call the 'affect of democracy' within the assemblies that people found most appealing. Being listened to and taken seriously by others while taking collective control over an important political moment really can be life-changing. This radically participative element, along with taking collective action, did most to increase people's collective capacities. It was this that produced such a strong identification with the process of the general assemblies, as Quinn Norton, a journalist who spent several months participating in the occupations across the US, makes clear.

The GA [general assembly] process also became part of everyday life: the queue, called 'stack'; the people's mic; consensus; arguments and counter arguments; points of information; blocking. Fights and logistical problems fell into little GAs, and the GA became a way of organizing thought. Hand gestures, called twinkles in New York, let groups express their feelings in silence. All of it migrated into the culture of camp life. After a while in the camps, you put your concerns 'on stack', and you twinkled people in conversation as a phatic. At first, like so many parts of Occupy, it was a wonder to see.[23]

The early exhilaration of participation in consensus-driven assemblies overlapped with an ideology of prefigurative proceduralism, also inherited from the alter-globalization movement, in which adherence to the correct organizational process could act as the point of unity and stand in for an assumed political commonality. This combination produced what I would call assemblyism, the idea that the general assembly is the direct and sufficient answer to the demand for 'Real Democracy Now!'[24] Just as some council communists in the twentieth century thought they had discovered in workers' councils the organizational form of a future communist society, some in Occupy, and beyond, mistook consensus assemblies, which had emerged from quite specific circumstance and inheritances, for a new universal model of democracy, which at the very least prefigured the post-capitalist society to come.

There was in this a failure to see how the needs of the conjuncture were forcing the general assemblies to adopt functions for which the consensus process wasn't designed. It was this that eventually turned the assemblies into a farce. As with all ideal types, a disconnect from the historical conditions from which they emerged set the model up to fail. As the limits of usefulness were reached, complete rejection ensued. This dynamic is quite visible in Norton's continuing testimony:

> Because the GA had no way to reject force, over time it fell to force. Proposals won by intimidation; bullies carried the day. What began as a way to let people reform and remake themselves had no mechanism for dealing with them when they didn't. It had no way to deal with parasites and predators. It became a diseased process, pushing out the weak and quiet it had meant to enfranchise until it finally collapsed when nothing was left but predators trying to rip out each other's throats. . . .
>
> The idea of the GA – its process, its form, inclusiveness – failed. It had all the best chances

to evolve, imprinted on the consciousness of thousands of occupiers like a second language. No idea gets a better chance than that, and it still failed.[25]

Rather than seeing the general assemblies, and so the movements of 2011, as a failure because they reached their limits of scalability, we should see them as a necessary moment in the emergence of a new political generation. The assemblies inadvertently ended up fulfilling the consciousness-raising functions that were so prominent in the 1970s. This makes sense to me for two reasons. Firstly, it seems that consciousness raising is a vital opening moment in class formation in situations in which there's no shared mass workplaces to fulfil the role of aggregation. The consciousness-raising groups of the 1970s feminist movement were used to compose 'women as a class' by overcoming the isolation of women, and the relegation of their problems into the private sphere. Secondly, we need to overcome neoliberalism's techniques of consciousness deflation. The individualizing effects of neoliberal governance and debt mean that some form of consciousness raising is a crucial step. The assemblies were a necessary moment, but they weren't sufficient. Many of the mechanisms of consciousness deflation built in the neoliberal era involved changing material conditions, which puts them out of reach of a mere 'revolution in the head'. These also undermined the sustainability of the protest camps. The all-or-nothing intensity required for full participation in that model of protest rubs up against our lack of free time as our lives are filled up by demoralizing work and dissatisfying distraction. The general assemblies and protest camps might allow the recognition of commonality and begin the search for structural causes, but they can't, on their own, overcome those structures.

Some of the most sophisticated campaigns to emerge from the 2011 wave retained the consciousness-raising functions of the assembly form as a first step in attacking mechanisms of control such as debt. The Strike Debt campaign targeting medical debt and student loans is one example that emerged from Occupy Wall Street.[26] One of the key pieces of advice Strike Debt gives to those wanting to initiate an anti-debt campaign is to hold debt assemblies, at which people testify publicly about their indebtedness to recognize their commonality and overcome their guilt. The same is true of the immensely powerful Spanish group Plataforma de Afectados por la Hipoteca (PAH) (Platform for People Affected by Mortgages), who use assemblies to 'realize the collective dimension of the problem and that there are structural elements that have influenced our decisions'.[27]

Campaigns like this were attempts to move from the symbolic leverage of the protest camps to exercising material leverage directly upon the structures and mechanisms cramping people's lives. Effective though these were, they increasingly encountered the problem of repression. Much of the Arab Spring fell victim to counter-revolution or civil war, while the Spanish government made much protest activity, and even the expression of dissent, illegal. The attempt to route around parliamentary democracy through the exercise of extra-parliamentary forms of power came up against the problem of the State's ability to set the conditions within which political activity takes place. Generation Left was born within explosive extra-parliamentary movements, yet all around the world between 2014 and 2016 these movements turned towards electoral politics.

In some countries, such as Spain, the generation of 2011 was large enough to create a new political common sense vying for dominance in the sphere of formal politics. In the UK the long 2011, which ran from the 2010 student movement, through Occupy, to the August 2011 riots, formed a much smaller generation but one that stayed highly internally networked. Despite its relatively small size it was able to facilitate the take-over of the Labour Party by the Left because it could act in a more cohesive fashion than any other sector. This electoral turn doesn't prove that 2011 failed. Quite the opposite: it proves it was successful. The unanimity with which the shift took place across many different countries in such a short period is the greatest proof that 2011 produced what Mannheim would call a Left generational unit on an international scale.

4

The Electoral Turn

For some reason an interview I watched in the early 1990s has stuck with me. It involved a story of a football manager introducing the more patient, continental style of football to players used to the directly attacking nature of the English leagues. During a training session the manager asked his attackers to pass and move in the final third of the pitch instead of launching the usual early cross into the box. After five minutes the centre forward piped up: 'What was the point of all that running, we're back in the same positions as we started?' 'Yes,' said the manager, 'but the defenders aren't.'[1]

I was reminded of this as the 2011 wave ebbed. What was the point of all that struggle when neoliberal governments still reign? The impact of such moments can initially be hard to see. Much of it takes place in the opaque realm of desires, expectations and the sense of what's possible. Those involved in the events of 2011, and those inspired by them, formed the cohesive core of a new international Left generation. The developments of that year formed what Mannheim would call a generational unit, and they appeared to all learn the same lesson at the same time, taking a distinct turn towards electoral politics. In 2011 many commentators looked at the protest camps and assemblies, and the horizontalist pronouncements coming from them, and thought the politics of the new generation was settled. That turned out not to be true. The new generational style of politics could not be equated, in any simple or literal way, with the slogans and practices of the square occupations. Similarly, we shouldn't mistake Jeremy Corbyn's manifesto or the campaign pitch of Bernie Sanders for the end point of this generation's politics. The explosions of 2011 and the electoral turn that followed must be seen as two waves of a generation on a longer political journey. Each phase provides its own clues to the style and underlying direction of the new politics, but they each need disentangling from the generational dynamics in which they're caught.

The electoral turn presented the core of Generation Left with a two-fold task. The first was to hegemonize the much larger 2008 generation made up of those disgruntled by contemporary conditions but, owing in part to those conditions, disinclined to engage in activist movements. The 2011 generation needed to produce an expression of their politics that resonated with the 2008 generation. In this there have been some successes. The new generational style parsed through the electoral and institutional spheres has proven attractive to the young and, as in some polls we are talking about the under 47s, the relatively young. This has allowed political distinctions between generations to be extended and registered. But this also reveals the second problem. To achieve lasting political change the new generation must work out how to ally with or overcome other political generations and age cohorts.

It's easy to date the 2011 wave of protest as it spread like lightning from country to country. Dating the electoral turn is more difficult because differing national electoral schedules delay the speed of contagion. There were indications of an electoral turn much earlier, but Thursday, 22 May 2014, was when it became apparent. In the European elections that day the Greek party of the radical Left, SYRIZA, leapt above the right-wing New Democracy party, gaining the most votes and all but wiping out the now neoliberalized former social democratic party PASOK, whose vote collapsed from 36 per cent to just 8 per cent. The fate of PASOK has since been repeated by neoliberalized 'centre Left' parties across Europe. This has benefited the Right but also cleared space for the radical Left. The other big story of the European elections came from Spain, where the Left populist party Podemos gained 8 per cent of the total national vote and five seats in the European Parliament. This was an astonishing result as the party had been set up just two months earlier.

Early the next year, on 25 January 2014, SYRIZA supporters gathered in a large marquee in Athens to watch the results of the Parliamentary elections. Mixed in with the crowd were leftists from around Europe, many drawn by links established during the alter-globalization movement 15 years earlier. What they witnessed, with SYRIZA gaining over 36 per cent of the vote, 149 seats in a 300-seat parliament and going on to become the governing party of Greece, both stunned and delighted them. For many this seemed to mark a definitive moment for European anti-neoliberal movements, who would now leave behind one stage of development and enter a new one. With Podemos also riding high in the polls it appeared that the movements had finally escaped their cycle of explosive impotence, in which serial social movements exhausted themselves against the impermeability of neoliberal governance.

As the year progressed, this neat narrative crumbled as the classic neoliberal anti-democratic mechanism of debt was used to derail the SYRIZA government's programme. The crunch point came with the so-called '*Oxi*' referendum called by SYRIZA to reassert its democratic mandate. The European Central Bank responded by provoking a run on the Greek banks to provoke a crisis and shock the population into line. The referendum asked whether to accept the hardline neoliberal austerity policies of the so-called Troika of creditors (the European Central Bank, the European Commission and the International Monetary Fund). The Greek people voted *Oxi* (No). Two-thirds of 'No' voters were under 30.[2] The Troika indicated they would ignore this result and, facing a disorderly exit from the euro, the SYRIZA government folded, implementing policies twice rejected by the Greek population. The failure of the Greek experiment was a pedagogical moment. Neoliberal reforms aim to prevent any return to social democracy through the simple act of electing a social democratic government. SYRIZA found itself in government but not in power. But even at their point of failure electoral politics can be useful if they can clarify the anti-democratic effects of neoliberalism that work against all forms of collective action.

The next key electoral test for Podemos after the 2014 European elections came with the Spanish municipal and regional elections held on 24 May 2015. The results of the regional elections suggested that the Podemos star was waning. They received only 13.5 per cent of the vote, far below their opinion poll high a couple of months earlier. The municipal elections, however, complicated this picture. Podemos did not run in these but offered support instead to the citizens' platforms that were forming in every major Spanish town and city. These platforms followed the model set by Guanyem Barcelona, later renamed Barcelona en Comú, a coalition of existing Left parties, initiatives and movement organizations closely tied to the spirit of 15M and the ongoing social movements around issues of social reproduction. It was these citizens' platforms that were the real winners on election night, taking control of four out of the five largest cities in Spain. The headline wins were by Ada Colau, the former spokesperson of anti-eviction campaign PAH, who was elected Mayor of Barcelona, and Manuela Carmena, an anti-corruption judge, who was elected the Mayor of the capital for the group Ahora Madrid.

We can see the citizens' platforms as part of an astute strategy to embed the Podemos leadership within an ecology of movements, initiatives and Left parties that might impede the pull towards the Right that comes with a national electoral politics that requires engagement with a mass media made tendentially right-wing by the economics of ownership and advertising. Spain offers the clearest example of the continuities between 2011 and the electoral turn. If the demand for 'Real Democracy Now!' was at first accompanied by the practice of the assemblies, then the electoral turn was 'a recognition that, as movements kept running up against the limits imposed by an unresponsive and increasingly repressive political system, the state *also* had to become a site of struggle – as a condition in fact, for movements to be able to continue their work'.[3]

Over the last few years 2011 has tended to disappear behind the subsequent electoral turn. This has obscured the continuities involved, but it's still possible to detect some of the participative ethic of 2011 in each iteration of electoralism. This suggests that, far from a reversal of direction, we are seeing the continuation of the same project through a different mode of politics. Of course, these modes aren't neutral; they exercise different forms of power and so have different affordances. It's possible, then, that the shift towards electoral politics will disrupt the commonalities of Generation Left. Not only do differing electoral cycles impose their own rhythms, but different electoral systems and political histories also provide different opportunities for Generation Left's involvement.

The 'First Past the Post' electoral system of the US and the UK makes the emergence of new parties more difficult. As a result, the electoral turn has taken place there within already existing parties. Bernie Sanders came close to gaining the US Democratic Party's Presidential nomination in a campaign driven by the young, while Jeremy Corbyn not only succeeded in becoming the most left-wing leader in the history of the Labour Party but also came close to winning the 2017 UK election. This was one of the most dramatic elections in British history. Corbyn confounded the polls and increased Labour's support by 20 per cent from the start of the campaign, finishing just two points behind the Conservatives. It was a campaign unlike any other in recent Labour history, displaying evidence of the participative, collaborative ethic of 2011. As the staff at Labour HQ were, on the whole, hostile to Corbyn's leadership and running a defensive operation aiming to minimize the losses they thought were coming, much of the actual campaigning took place outside formal party structures. Groups of people self-organized canvassing campaigns using apps such as 'My Nearest Marginal' produced by the Corbyn-supporting group Momentum, while much of the most effective communication came from the viral spread of videos and memes created independently from the party machinery. It was the complete opposite of the tightly controlled message discipline of the New Labour years. Corbyn himself focused on touring the country, drawing huge crowds to his rallies. This dynamic peaked in May with the spontaneous emergence of the 'Oh, Jeremy Corbyn' chant during his appearance at a music festival in Prenton Park football stadium.

The paradox of the electoral turn in the UK and US is the ability of political leaders over the age of 65 to enthuse primarily young people to join political parties and movements. Jeremy Corbyn was 68 when he fought the general election, and Bernie Sanders campaigned for the Democratic nomination for the US Presidential election aged 74. I'd suggest that Corbyn and Sanders are attractive to the young because they are seen as untainted by the cynicism and corruption of the last 30 years of representative politics. They hark back to, and in fact date back to, traditions of less complicated and self-serving political commitment. Indeed, both Corbyn and Sanders trade on their reputations as political leaders who refused to compromise their beliefs. The cohort of politicians that's missing from this alliance are those in the 35 to 60 age range – those we can call the Third Way Left generation.

Generational Blind Spots

As the electoral turn in the UK and US took place within political parties controlled by the neoliberal Third Way centrists, they provide the clearest examples of the mode of interaction between these two Left generations.[4] In the US the generational dynamic was masked at first by an articulation of gender. Despite age being by far the clearest point of divergence in support for Sanders and Clinton, the attempt was made to cast support for the former as having an anti-feminist flavour. The phrase 'Bernie Bros' was used by Clinton supporters to obscure the generational dynamic, but although Clinton led Sanders 61 per cent to 37 per cent among female voters overall, Sanders led Clinton by 37 per cent among 18- to 29-year-old women.[5]

In the UK the denial of a generational dynamic has taken on even more outrageous proportions. From the moment of Corbyn's election as Labour leader 'centrist' political commentators in alliance with MPs on the right of the Labour Party and a right-wing press have waged an unrelenting campaign to undermine and overturn his leadership. The commentariat have not just been uncomprehending of young people's turn to the Left, they have been boastfully disinterested to the point of denial.[6] The *Financial Times* columnist Janan Ganesh tweeted: 'All this stuff about Corbyn and this so-called movement. The truth is they're just as thick as pig shit.'[7] Ganesh is on the centre Right, but there was no more appetite for analysis of this novel political phenomenon among the centrist Third Way Left. The *Observer* columnist Nick Cohen wrote, '[C]ultism has turned Labour into a childish, sycophantic, thuggish and unthinking party.'[8] His vicious condescension was not out of the ordinary. *Guardian* columnist Hadley Freeman even went so far as to compare support for Corbyn to the homicidal cultism of the Charles Manson Family.[9]

How do we explain the excessiveness of these denunciations? They go way beyond simple political disagreement or even lazy disinterest. A generational analysis can provide some insight. The Brazilian philosopher and activist Rodrigo Nunes argues that Left generations tend to form in the blind spots of their predecessors, particularly when the latter has held power in the lead-up to the emergence of the former.[10] In the case of Generation Left the socio-economic problems that became crystallized in 2008 and politicized in 2011 are legacies of a time when the Third Way neoliberal centrists were in government across much of the developed world. It makes sense that the new generation would form in opposition to those governments and focus on problems that the governing party can't or won't address. Yet there is more to this moment of generational non-communication than a simple dynamic of opposition.

The Third Way is a Left generation, even if its defining characteristic has been to move to the Right. It was catalysed by the event of 1989: the Fall of the Berlin Wall and the subsequent great doubling of the global labour force. The constriction of possibility this event produced finally decided the battles of the 1980s and persuaded a generation of leftists that it was no longer possible to move society in a leftwards direction. This premise informs the rest of the coordinates of the Third Way world-view. If the existing balance of forces could not be changed, then progressive politics had to find a new strategy. This entailed maintaining, and indeed further entrenching, the hegemony of finance capital and adopting what New Labour strategist Peter Mandelson famously called an 'intensely relaxed' attitude to the dramatic concentration of wealth among a tiny elite. The trade-off for this accommodation was the modest redistribution of wealth achieved by diverting a portion of the tax received from a buoyant financial and housing sector towards the working poor. Yet this redistribution would come on a firmly neoliberal basis with public spending funnelled through private provision and aligned with the spread of neoliberal modes of governance. The US version of the Third Way, seen most clearly in the tenure of President Clinton, was even more regressive. Welfare provision was rolled back and the carceral system massively expanded to replace it.

The common-sense politics of the Third Way era consisted of only one move: tack Right to win over 'centrist' swing voters. Such was the consistency with which this model was deployed that it became divorced from the conditions that produced it and mistaken for permanent political wisdom. While this strategy appeared to work in the 1990s, at least on its own terms, it ultimately contained a self-defeating logic. Adopting right-wing policies and narratives ends up strengthening the Right and undermining the Left's bases of support. The financial crash of 2008 saw these pigeons come home to roost. The centre Left has been punished for the crisis far more than the centre Right. The neoliberal model of growth which allowed some redistribution of the proceeds of finance has gone for good and the political coalitions built by the centre Left have vanished with it. But the problem runs deeper than that. In recent years it has often appeared to be Jeremy Corbyn's capture of the Labour Party that centrists want to repudiate, or Bernie Sanders' capture of the youth vote. But behind those events is the crisis of 2008. It's this event that produces an existential crisis for centrists because it works backwards through history to reveal the economic growth that took place during their highpoint to have always been illusory. The event of 2008 retrospectively robs the Third Way Left of its apparent achievements.

The common sense of Generation Left sits slap-bang in a place that the Third Way's presuppositions prevent it from seeing. Driven by the meagreness of its economic prospects and learning from the Third Way's failure, Generation Left aims for an irrevocable transformation of the balance of forces in favour of the working class. Corbyn's policy of abolishing student fess was castigated as regressive by centrists because poorer groups could better use those resources. It's a critique that fails to see the role that student fees and debt plays in training neoliberal subjects. The Third Way Left can't see Generation Left because recognizing the existence of a new Left generation means accepting that their analytical grid can no longer make sense of the world. Non-political, and indeed paranoid, concepts such as 'cultism', with its connotations of the kind of mesmerism by a leader found in early right-wing crowd theory, are used to close the gap between a calcified world-view and phenomena that no longer accord with it. It's this that explains the excessive acting out of the commentariat. Articles like Hadley Freeman's are not meant to persuade. They are the existential reassertion of generational relevance. 'We are REAL REAL REAL!!! ... [they shout] as they feel ... reality slipping away from them.'[11]

Escaping Left Melancholy

If accommodation with neoliberalism was the response of the Third Way Left, then the long 1989 affected the radical Left in other ways. Writing in

1999, and so commenting on the Left's 'failure to apprehend the character of the age and to develop a political critique and a moral-political vision appropriate to this character',[12] Wendy Brown offers the following description of the consequences.

> What emerges is a Left that operates without either a deep and radical critique of the status quo or a compelling alternative to the existing order of things . . . a Left that has become more attached to its impossibility than to its potential fruitfulness, a Left that is most at home dwelling not in hopefulness but in its own marginality and failure, a Left that is thus caught in a structure of melancholic attachment to a certain strain of its own dead past, whose spirit is ghostly, whose structure of desire is backward looking and punishing.[13]

Brown calls this attitude Left Melancholy. She takes the phrase from Walter Benjamin, who, writing in the 1930s, was himself experiencing a bleak time for the Left. In turn Benjamin takes the concept of melancholy from Freud's distinction between it and mourning. If a Left generation could recognize and mourn the passing of the world in which it had traction, then it could move on and engage the world as it is now. Melancholy, on the other hand, denotes an attachment to the object of one's sorrowful loss [which] supersedes any desire to recover from this loss, to live free of it in the present, to be unburdened by it. This is what renders melancholia a persistent condition, a state, indeed, a structure of desire, rather than a transient response to death or loss.[14]

Melancholia can, then, be the mode through which a farcical repetition of the traditions of past generations presents itself, as people get 'attached more to a particular political analysis or ideal – even to the failure of that ideal – than to seizing possibilities for radical change in the present'.[15] But aspects of Left Melancholy can also mark a period in which the potential for change diminishes. Much radical politics and theory through the 1990s contained the implicit presupposition that not only was radical change not on the immediate agenda but that also there would never be a mass audience for such ideas.

We can even see traces of Left Melancholy in the alter-globalization movement, the first political generation to attempt to produce the political forms of a post-neoliberal Left. That generation was brought into being by the event of Seattle 1999, a successful blockade of a World Trade Organization summit in the city. It sparked a classic moment of excess in which summit protests, convergence camps and social forums spread around the world. However, the movement soon settled down into a yearly repetition of very similar events. This cadence could reproduce a movement, but it couldn't change the world. The most popular slogan of the time, 'Another World is Possible', was meant as a refutation of the neoliberal slogan 'There is No Alternative', yet there was little serious discussion of how to bring that possible world into actual existence. In retrospect we can see that the event of 1999 produced a generation that failed to escape the gravitational pull of 1989, that black hole of possibility.

Wendy Brown calls Left Melancholy 'a structure of desire'. It's a compulsive loop that the animating desires of the Left can fall into. But desires are produced by external forces as much as internal ones. One big difference between the alter-globalization cycle and the current circulation of struggle is the confidence of the neoliberal enemy, so high in 1999 but devastated by 2008. Left Melancholy can't be overcome by simply changing your perspective, although this can sometimes help; rather it takes the working through and overcoming of the material structures and practices that limit our ability to understand and act in the world. The high points of the electoral turn show there is an audience for Left ideas. Left theory must be revolutionized by this realization. But more than this, we have glimpsed the very real possibility of Generation Left becoming hegemonic among young people. This is the starting point for reopening the question of strategy. It isn't, however, strategy's end point.

Growing an Ecology

If movements and their initiating events often exceed the current sense of what's possible, then electoral politics tends to face in the other direction. The forces acting in the electoral realm all point towards a compromise with the existing sense of possibility. The art of the possible. While individual electoral events, an election campaign or referendum, can produce moments of excess, the day-to-day conduct of electoral politics pulls to the Right. Winning elections involves building social coalitions, which must always entail some compromise, but the central role played by mass media means we fight on enemy territory. And the media are merely the first line of defence. Left governments will also need to overcome an obstreperous civil service, allay the threat of coups, both soft and hard, and prepare for a confrontation with international capital. The great question facing left-wing governments in our time is what to do when capital goes on strike. This can take the form of capital flight, a refusal to invest or an attack on the currency big enough to turn off the ATMs.

Resolving any of these problems requires a mobilized population. Only movements can counteract the media's attempts to provoke a sense of crisis and shock. Only movements acting directly to improve people's lives can bring about the deep social change we require. And only the exercise of extra-parliamentary forms of power can counter the power of capital. There are two forms such power can take. The first is the power to prevent the functioning of business as usual. A strike throughout society, a social strike, to counter the threat of a capital strike.[16] The second is the power to do things differently. Developing the commons, the collaborative sector and solidarity economies. Greece has a dense network of projects addressing the crisis of social reproduction at some degree of autonomy from capital and the State. These self-organized health clinics, community kitchens and supermarkets acted as a kind of shock absorber against intimidation from the European Central Bank.

The problem with this dual strategy is that electoral politics has strong tendencies towards demobilizing and eliding all other modes of politics. It imposes its own temporality of electoral cycles which don't fit the temporality of movements. And representative politics inevitably involves specialists taking action on behalf of others in a rarefied environment to which only they have access.

In many ways, this fits present circumstances. The material conditions for sustained mass political engagement are not yet in place. For most, political action is only achievable episodically and electoral politics is episodic, requiring mass campaigning at key points in the cycle. Yet even here there are difficulties keeping Generation Left engaged enough to win the smaller electoral battles. Extra-parliamentary politics must also learn this lesson and orientate itself around episodic mass engagement even as we attempt to alter the conditions that necessitate it.

The Left needs an ecosystem of organizations fulfilling different functions and acting sympathetically towards each other without one subsuming the others. We need what Nick Srnicek and Alex Williams call 'a functional complementarity between organisations'.[17] So far Generation Left has shown an admirable ability to overcome the fetishization of specific organizational forms, riding one until its limits are reached, then changing vehicles to go further. Now, however, it needs to attend to several functions at once to head off the predictable ill effects of the electoral turn. Electoral projects must be encircled by movements, think tanks, municipal projects and a network of autonomous organizations. As President Franklin Roosevelt is reported to have said to radical labour leaders, 'I agree with you, I want to do it, now make me do it.' In turn Left governments must seek to devolve power outwards, to undermine their own centralization of power, to be 'in and against the State'.[18]

In this project Generation Left can find key allies and resources in those veterans of past Left generations who are regenerating themselves through non-farcical repetitions of their own traditions. As Mannheim says, '[I]t occurs very frequently that the nucleus of the attitudes particular to the new generation is first developed by older people who are isolated in their own generation.'[19] Luckily, the current generation seems predisposed to evade Left Melancholy. Generation Left is the first generation for whom the failures and impasses of the twentieth-century Left are an inheritance rather than lived experience. The first post-Cold War generation are not afraid of the words 'socialism' and 'communism'; they are reinventing them and their traditions in their own image. There is, however, another problem for the Left to face: the generational gap in politics revealed by right-wing electoral triumphs. It's to this that we turn in the final chapter.

5

Reinventing Adulthood

Overheard on a train. Two work colleagues in awkward conversation. One young, one a lot older and obviously more senior. They're struggling for things to talk about. The younger one says: 'Did you watch that TV programme *Black Mirror* last night?' Older one replies, 'No, I don't like it.' Younger colleague struggles to keep the conversation alive, 'I just find them quite thought provoking.' Older colleague retorts, 'Yes, but I don't want my thoughts provoked.' The conversation dribbled on. It turned out the older man was a fan of *Top Gear*.

Is there something inherent in ageing that leads to conservatism in cultural tastes, in social views, in political outlook? Will those in today's Generation Left inevitably turn into sour-faced, right-wing curmudgeons? Or is there a way to escape that fate?

Why is Conservatism So Old?

Getting older inevitably involves some accretion. As you collect experiences, habits and familiarities, they begin to stick to you. This process tends to slow you down and reduces your room for manoeuvre. In part, this comes from the responsibilities of work and family, but not all encumbrances are to be rejected. Every parent has had to walk across a room with a young child clinging to their leg, but most would trade some mobility for a little unconditional love. Accretion turns problematic because our current model of adulthood causes sedimentation. Our habitual lives get turned into concrete.

Some accretion is central to Mannheim's concept of political generations. Younger people have a different, more intense relationship to formative events because they have yet to build up a sedimented habitus. Older generations, on the other hand, tend to interpret new events through the perceived lessons of their own formative experiences. If an event is of a big enough scale, then the different ways in which that event is received can produce distinct generational outlooks. People tend to adopt their baseline views in their youth and these can get out of kilter with wider social mores. As society became more 'socially liberal' through the second half of the twentieth century and into the twenty-first, people could appear to become more conservative as they aged without their actual views changing at all. So at least some of the basis for the idea that ageing makes you more conservative rests on a category error. Generational effects are being mistaken for life-cycle effects. But, of course, this historical trend towards 'socially liberal' attitudes is not inevitable. People have had to fight for increased equality around race, gender and sexuality. As I've made clear from the start of the book, political genera-tions are intimately entwined with the dynamics of class struggle.

Beyond this generational effect there remains a life-cycle trend in the data. In fact the conservatism of older people has become a much more pro-nounced trend in recent years. Yet the very fact that this trend alters over history should throw doubt on the idea that it's a natural law. The conservatism of the elderly seems socially constructed as much as something inherent in our physiology. The extent to which one or the other predominates is an old debate, but in recent times it's likely to be framed in terms of neural plasticity. The brains of the young, the theory goes, are more adept at making new neural connections and therefore more likely to take on new ideas and experiences. Yet even this rule is not set in stone. Brain plasticity is affected by lifestyle and, in particular, by our habitual levels of intellectual activity and encounters with novel experiences. It's hard for us to detach the decline of brain plasticity among the elderly from the modern model of adulthood and ageing which reinforces it through social isolation. The active social life associated with youth is expected to decline in adulthood as we withdraw into a familiar job and a nuclear family. This isolation is concretized in the layout of our cities and the structure of our housing. Even the dominant technologies of the twentieth century, the car and the television, facilitate domesticated separation. This all helps produce conservative social views.

As areas have become increasingly segregated by age as well as race and class, it is the young who have ended up more ethnically and culturally diverse. They're more likely to live in the multicultural cities while the elderly are less likely to encounter those of different races and backgrounds. A lack of relevant personal experience makes you more susceptible to the media's framing of an issue, and as the press is predominantly owned by oligarchs, it is tendentially right-wing. The fact that racism is most prevalent in less racially mixed areas supports this proposition. Indeed, patterns of media consumption are also heavily divided by age. Increasingly only the elderly buy newspapers. Without countervailing mechanisms, the press also sets the agenda for television news. There's little doubt that the right-wing press, along with most broadcast news, have business models based on the mobilization of fear. Events such as Brexit or Trump are not reducible to this fact, but they aren't explainable without it. Yet the heart of the matter is this: people are susceptible to such mobilization because they fear dispossession.

In their recent book *Assembly* Michael Hardt and Antonio Negri argue: 'Private property promises to connect you in community but instead merely provides shelter by separating you from others, defending you from the hordes. ... Scratch the surface of private property's veneer of security and you will find the real foundation: fear. The society of private property manages and propagates fear.'[1] Fear is inherent in private property. The fear that someone will come and take away your property has animated conservatism from its inception. But property ownership on a mass scale is a relatively recent affair and, judging by declining rates of home ownership among the young, it increasingly looks like a temporary one.

The current model of adulthood is based around the form of private property. Yet there is nothing natural about this. It's the result of much effort by serial political projects. The link between adulthood and property ownership has long roots in the history of capitalism and the liberal political theory that has accompanied it. For Locke, among others, both the enclosure of the commons and colonial expropriation were justified by the supposed 'child-like' incapacity of the land's original users to develop their 'property' to its full potential.[2] Similarly, the history of property qualifications on suffrage provides another example of how the rights and responsibilities of adulthood have been tied to property ownership. This is not ancient history. Property restrictions on voting were only fully lifted in the UK in 1928, while extra votes for owners of multiple properties were not abolished until 1948. The advent of universal adult suffrage provoked a crisis in the conservative project. The idea of 'a property-owning democracy' emerged out of this crisis, with the diffusion of private property ownership seen as a counter to the forms of collective property advocated by socialists. This project only reached full fruition with the neoliberal reforms to finance and the housing market in the 1980s and 1990s.[3] As a consequence, the interests of a decisive proportion of the electorate have been aligned with finance. The crash of 2008 taught us, however, that property ownership is an insecure means of securing your future. It loses its value in a crisis just when you need it most. In the end, as Hardt and Negri put it, 'Property won't save you.'[4] The current model of adulthood and ageing has real drawbacks for those caught within it. It's a machine for producing isolated, fearful subjects who descend into loneliness on an epidemic level in old age. There are very real risks that this will be the basis for a catastrophic turn to the Far Right. But the biggest evidence that the model is broken lies elsewhere. It has simply stopped taking new members.

Adulthood isn't Working

Young people are finding it increasingly hard to attain the markers of successful adulthood. Traditionally, these included getting a 'proper job' – a settled place in the economy – getting married, becoming a parent and, increasingly over the last 40 years, owning your own home. Each one of these has become more difficult to achieve or has been pushed back much later in life owing, in part, to material insecurity. The prevalence of low-wage, precarious and temporary employment has turned a stable place in the economy into a pipe-dream for many, while people are getting married and having children later in life, if at all. By 2015, for instance, British people got married an average of nearly 10 years later than they did in 1970.[5] In the US it's a similar story: there have been 4.8 million fewer children born there than pre-crisis trends predicted.[6] These changes are driven partly by women's increasing participation in the labour force, along with the increased acceptability of alternative family arrangements, but the economic difficulties and uncertainties that have followed the financial crash have caused an involuntary acceleration of these trends.[7] When the crisis started in 2008, one in five of 20- to 34-year-olds still lived with their parents in the UK; by 2015 this was up to one in four.[8] Even more startlingly, levels of home ownership among young British adults have more than halved in 20 years.[9]

Of course, these markers were never universally available or necessarily desirable, but their decline still indicates an adulthood in crisis. The solutions that are usually offered suggest removing the blockages preventing young people from moving into adulthood. I don't think this is possible: class composition has changed, but more than this, any attempt to follow that path courts disaster by setting up a generational zero-sum game. If property prices are made more affordable – by building more houses, for example – this will have to come at the cost of older generations, whose security in old age is tied into the property bubble. A generational clash like this needs to be sidestepped. We need to break the alignment between pensioners and finance to reveal the real class antagonists this alliance is obscuring. That means finding new ways of guaranteeing material security in old age. At the same time the idea of attaining a liveable pension while still fit enough to enjoy it seems implausible to most people under 30. Each stage of the life-cycle is broken or in the process of breaking. The whole thing needs reinventing.[10] This may seem a huge task, but the social engineering of neoliberalism was on a similar order of scale. Indeed, we don't have to start our own project from scratch. The counterculture of the 1960s and 1970s, with its experiments in collective living and feminist critiques of the nuclear family, can be seen as an attempt to reinvent adulthood around egalitarian principles while imbuing it with at least some of the freedom of youth. Although those experiments were largely defeated in the 1980s, they contain models that could still be re-explored. But any attempts to reform adulthood around the affects of 'youth' face a real difficulty today. Young people no longer have access to many of the experiences and properties that we associate with it.

Blocked Youth

Our contemporary conception of youth, as a socio-economic category separate from childhood and adulthood, is a relatively recent invention. It began to develop in the early twentieth century but only became a mass phenomenon after the Second World War. Rising mass affluence relieved the pressure for young people to earn money for the family, allowing the consumption patterns of youth markets to develop their own dynamics. Starting with the invention of the 'teenager' in 1944, this reached its apotheosis with the youth culture of the 1960s and 1970s – the previous era when age was a key point of political division.[11] During those decades 'youth' become associated with freedom and self-reinvention. It became a period of relative freedom from the parental family, but preceded the full embrace of the discipline of adulthood, a permanent job and the responsibilities of raising one's own family. At that time 'youth' seemed like a category that cut across and undermined class affinities. With hindsight, we can see the youth movement as a symptom of a shift in class composition. The high wages and State-backed social security of the era provided the material and psychic security that enabled young people's exploration of freedom. As the era went on, the counterculture tried to spread the properties of 'youth' across the whole of life. The neoliberal counter-revolution destroyed these experiments by reasserting the link between private property and adulthood. As home ownership was the central inducement, the restoration of the nuclear family followed in its wake.

Do young people still experience 'youth' as a time of self-reinvention and freedom? The time and space available to them certainly seems diminished. We've already seen how student and youth debt brings forward the responsibilities of a supposed future adulthood which then colonizes the present. Astronomical property prices, low wages, student fees and the elimination of unemployment benefit have severely squeezed the traditional means through which young people gain time free from work. Young adults are trapped working long hours at badly paid jobs just to make enough money to pay the rent. That costs the average 18- to 36-year-old over a third of their post-tax income. In the 1960s and 1970s their grandparents spent just 5–10 per cent of income on housing. Indeed, the un-freedom of *Generation Rent* doesn't just reveal the present circumstances of youth; it also provides a glimpse into a possible future model of adulthood.

The lives of the young are dominated by rent. It's a relation that stretches far beyond housing. The dominant business models of the age, and the ones young people are most likely to encounter, are based on extracting streams of rent. This is, of course, how debt works, but increasingly we rent access to the music we listen to, the television shows we watch and the cars we drive. The misnamed 'sharing economy' has spread renting into ever more areas of life. And underneath it all the biggest companies in the world rent access to the vital infrastructure of twenty-first-century life. It's becoming ever more clear that platform capitalism is an extractivist industry. The platform giants increasingly demand monetary rents but they all extract and take ownership of the data our interactions produce. The self-reinforcing dynamics of data collection, rent and debt, in which money and control all flow one way, are shifting us from property-owning democracy to oligarchic rentierism. The trend is neo-feudalist. Jeff Bezos and Mark Zuckerberg live like kings while the rest of us become indebted serfs. The hegemony of finance is maintained while property ownership is restricted and centralized. The idea of a property-owning democracy only emerged in response to the threat of socialism latent in mass suffrage. Oligarchic rent-ierism assumes this threat is gone, that democracy can be nullified by debt or managed into impotency. But if this assumption is wrong, if democracy can be reasserted and the corruptive power of the oligarchs defeated, then there are more desirable potentials latent in the current composition of class and the experiences of the young.

Everything for Everyone!

The value of private property is linked to scarcity. It has a rivalrous nature: either *you* have it or *I* have it. This inherent potential for dispossession is what makes property owners vulnerable to right-wing mobilizations of fear. If we can construct adulthood around the attributes of non-rivalrous property, then we can prevent those in Generation Left from turning Right as they age. Luckily, just such a form of common property is latent in our everyday lives. As Hardt and Negri argue, '[T]he dominant figures of property in the contemporary era – including code, images, cultural products, patents, knowledge, and the like – are largely immaterial and, more important, indefinitely reproducible.'[12] Immaterial property, most notably digital property, is non-rivalrous. The cost of producing one more copy is virtually nil. I can have it, you can have it and nobody loses out. So the natural price of digital property tends towards zero. Platform capitalism took a long time to develop because it had to overcome the spontaneous culture of the internet. The idea of a digital commons is intuitively grasped because it's so close to lived experience. Even the compulsive narcissism built into capitalist platforms like Facebook can't eliminate the remainder upon which it is based: the desire for sociality, self-expression, collective creation and autonomy. Generation Left is already primed for a remodelling of adulthood around the attributes of the commons.

Any programme for a commons-based adulthood must facilitate the re-emergence of the digital commons. This will involve incentivizing forms of collaborative production, disincentivizing business models based on rent, and socializing the benefits of automation, data creation and the positive externalities of network effects.[13] But if the commons is to overcome the lure of property ownership, it will have to also become dominant in the rest of life. Quite simple legal changes could restore the sharing economy to its original meaning. Platform

cooperatives could replace parasitic capitalist platforms such as Uber and Deliveroo if existing labour
law were applied with vigour. But the most vital
plank of any programme must be the massive
expansion of cooperative housing and the spread of
intergenerational co-housing.

This will no doubt take innovative forms of
public–commons partnerships in which the commons provides the direction of travel for institutional
reform.[14] The vital advantage of the commons over
most forms of public ownership is its intimate link
to participative democracy.[15] As Hardt and Negri
put it, 'The common stands in contrast to property
in a . . . radical way, by eliminating the character of
exclusion from the right of both use and decision-
making, instituting instead a schema of open shared
use and democratic governance.'[16] A commons is
not a free-for-all; it needs a community to tend and
govern it. Governing the commons is the diametric
opposite of neoliberal managerialism. It constitutes
a training in democracy. Instead of isolated, competitive and hierarchized individuals it produces more
connected, collaborative and powerful collectivities.
Even better, we don't have to wait until the Left seize
State power before we start this training. Powerful
solidarity networks and renters' unions, in which
participants pledge to back each other over disputes

with landlords and companies, can be built now. Along with the reinvigoration and democratization of the union movement they represent the missing elements of the new ecology of Left organizations that the electoral turn demands. They can also act as lessons not just in democratic governance but also in the basis of true security. Embedding in an active, democratic community is by far the most secure way of ensuring you will be cared for and your needs will be met. The security offered by private property is ephemeral in comparison.

Something similar is suggested, once again, by Hardt and Negri:

> We find a powerful foretaste of this real security, which neither private property nor the state can accomplish, in the forms of community and cooperation that emerge in the midst of social and ecological disaster. In recent years, for instance, from Brazil and Argentina to Spain, Greece and Japan, people have emerged from poverty and crisis to develop solidarity economies and organize production, incomes, services, food, and housing on a local scale. Solidarity economies emphasize cooperation and self-management as an alternative to the regime of profit and capitalist control, which is not only more egalitarian but also more efficient and stable.[17]

We face something like a Catch 22 in achieving this vision. At the moment, we have neither the time nor the resources to participate fully in democracy. As a result, most participate episodically, if at all. Yet a lack of participation ensures governments are run on behalf of the capitalists, who will always want to make us work harder and longer for less. It's a negative feedback loop. But if we can reach a democratic tipping point, we can get that circuit moving in the other direction. Raised consciousness will allow us the free time, resources and confidence to assert our interests; this should lead to more democracy and more resources from which to push further. It's the cycle the oligarchs fear most.

This will require experiments in State-provided universal basic income and universal basic services. The establishment of collective security against the threat of destitution through unemployment will relaunch serious countercultural experimentation in consciousness expansion and new ways of living. We will see renewed attempts to rediscover the connection between 'youth' and freedom along with attempts to spread that freedom into adult life. For young people stuck in precarious employment a job for life might sound like a luxury rather than a life sentence but it won't take much to swap this around. Mixing flexibility with security to produce control over work and life could mean nobody *needs* a stable place in the economy to become a responsible adult. Adulthood certainly needs some of the freedom of youth but it would be a mistake to collapse both ages into each other. Youth is a time of freedom partly owing to a lack of responsibilities. Growing into adulthood should involve more fully taking on the responsibilities that come with life, but those responsibilities need reformulating around an extended concept of care. The boundaries that surround who or what can be cared about need overcoming, but that can't be a task for mere individuals.

Deciding on the priorities of care, along with the attendant deployment of resources, is synonymous with politics. It's the reason we need an excess of democracy. When feminists say they want to smash the nuclear family, it's not because they want to stop caring for their loved ones. It's because they want to extend that bond of love to include others. The political composition of Generation Left demands a revaluation of care. Care and social reproductive work, paid and unpaid, is the fastest growing sector of labour. It's a trend that will accelerate as the automation of work advances. The care sector has also increasingly been the location of the largest and most militant industrial action. It's a trend that produces its own dilemmas of action: how do care workers strike without harming those they care for?[18] But it also reveals the terrible care deficit produced by the sociopathy of neoliberalism. The consciousness raising of Generation Left has taken the form of an iterative process of care and repair. It was evident in the super-therapeutic functions exercised through 2011's assemblies and it can be seen in the ongoing solidarity economies and experiments in collective practices of care.[19] Once the material and psychic resources have been assembled we need to direct this caring function towards the horrendous crisis in elderly care.

People always have a complex range of desires and interests. Which ones get acted upon depends on what seems possible. Changes in wider circumstances – what we've called the technical composition – set the background for attempts to recompose those interests along new lines of political potential. We've seen how changes in young people's material realities have closed off neoliberal aspiration, the previously dominant framing of the future. New alignments of interests have emerged in the wake. The underemployment of graduates, for example, is inclining them to find commonalities with non-graduate youths. A Left generational unit was formed in the crucible of 2011. Its task since then has been to turn the expansion of possibility it found there into a political project which can give direction to this new alignment of interests. The reinvention of adulthood around the attributes of the commons could help provide this direction. It takes existing tendencies and extends them with the aim of shaping the future field of political possibility. But it's not just about preventing Generation Left from turning Right in old age; it can also provide the horizon which orientates our attempts to bridge the generation gap today.

Although we won't completely break the hegemony of right-wing ideas among the elderly, we can certainly disrupt it and peel away a decisive minority. We simply need to weaken the alignment of their interests with finance capital and show a convincing potential for a different kind of old age. This will mean social security provided by the public and the commons to tempt the ageing out from behind the isolating walls of private property. But this promise will only be believed if intergenerational solidarity is also reflected in the movements, organizations and culture we build now. After all, the retired have much to offer Generation Left. They have, not least, that rarest of contemporary commodities, free time. The young, meanwhile, can offer sociality to help overcome the isolation and loneliness that plague old age. If political generations are seen purely as age-based, then the foundation for such a reconciliation becomes unclear, but if we recognize that the current generation gap is an effect of the recomposition of class, then shared class interests can be built to bridge the gap.

It's easy to rage at the Baby Boomers when we look at the regimes they've voted into power, but we must remember that this is simply what a defeated generation looks like. There was an incredibly powerful and hopeful Left generation ascending before its defeat by the neoliberal turn. That defeat has come at a huge price. And it's not just them or us who will pay it but countless generations to come. The coincidence of the discovery of climate change and the rise of neoliberalism has been catastrophic. The best opportunity to tackle global warming has been squandered. History will be most harsh on those who have embraced climate denial because they don't like the solutions but, owing to their age, won't face the worst consequences. We sit at a rare crossroads in history. Generation Left has to win and extended its ethic of care to the planetary commons. The future can't afford the defeat of another Left generation.

Notes

Chapter 1 Re: Generations

1 YouGov, 'How Britain Voted at the 2017 General Election': https://yougov.co.uk/news/2017/06/13/how-britain-voted-2017-general-election/.

2 Ipsos MORI, 'How Britain Voted in 2010': https://www.ipsos.com/ipsos-mori/en-uk/how-britain-voted-2010.

3 K. Kawashima-Ginsberg, N. Hyatt, A. Kiesa and F. Sullivan, *Donald Trump and Young Voters*, CIRCLE report, Tufts University, June 2016: https://civicyouth.org/wp-content/uploads/2016/06/Trump-and-Youth-Vote.pdf.

4 Quoted in M. Ehrenfreund, 'Bernie Sanders is Profoundly Changing How Millennials Think About Politics, Poll Shows', *Washington Post*, 25 April 2016: https://www.washingtonpost.com/news/wonk/wp/2016/04/25/bernie-sanders-is-profoundly-changing-how-millennials-think-about-politics-poll-shows/.

5 Harvard IOP Spring 2016 Poll: http://iop.harvard.
edu/youth-poll/harvard-iop-spring-2016-poll.

6 YouGov, 6–8 May 2015: http://cdn.yougov.com/
cumulus_uploads/document/3csd07d2dd/tabs_OPI_
socialism_20150508.pdf.

7 Among US Millennials, 31 per cent were doing the
same: https://info.marublue.net/acton/attachment/36
213/f-0012/1/-/-/-/-/BuzzFeed%20News.pdf.

8 B. Tulgan, *Not Everyone Gets a Trophy: How to
Manage Generation Y*, San Francisco, CA: Jossey-
Bass, 2009. J. Twenge, *Generation Me*, New York:
Atria Books, 2014.

9 B. Gardiner, *Stagnation Generation*, London:
Resolution Foundation, 2016.

10 Ibid., p. 7.

11 Ibid., p. 39.

12 N. Howe and W. Strauss, *Generations: The History
of America's Future, 1584 to 2069*, New York:
William Morrow, 1991.

13 N. Howe and W. Strauss, *Millennials Rising: The
Next Great Generation*, New York: Vintage, 2000,
pp. 7–9.

14 Thatcher uttered the infamous phrase in an interview
with *Woman's Own* magazine, 23 September 1987.

15 Gardiner *Stagnation Generation*, p. 17. In fact, there
have been several names proposed for this latest
generation, from Gen Z to iGen to post-Millennials.
There is, of course, no agreement on when this generation begins.

16 D. Willetts, *The Pinch*, London: Atlantic, 2010. In
2015 Willetts became executive chairman of the

Resolution Foundation, ensuring that his perspective has guided much research into intergenerational justice.

17 E. Howker and S. Malik, *Jilted Generation*, London: Icon, 2013, pp. 39–41.

18 Gardiner, *Stagnation Generation*, p. 39.

19 For discussion of the long wage stagnation and the falling wage share of national income see S. Lansley and H. Reed, *How to Boost the Wage Share*, London: TUC, 2013.

20 For a discussion of this process see W. Streeck, 'The Crises of Democratic Capitalism', *New Left Review*, 71 (2011): https://newleftreview.org/II/71/wolfgang-streeck-the-crises-of-democratic-capitalism, and W. Brown, *Undoing the Demos: Neoliberalism's Stealth Revolution*, New York: Zone Books, 2015.

21 K. Mannheim, 'The Problem of Generations', in *Essays on the Sociology of Knowledge*, London: Routledge, 1952, p. 309.

22 S. Žižek, *Event: Philosophy in Transit*, London: Penguin, 2014, p. 179.

23 Mannheim, 'The Problem of Generations', p. 303.

24 Ibid., p. 298.

25 Ibid., p. 308.

26 Ibid., p. 307.

27 Mannheim names this process the creation of a generational style or entelechy.

28 F. Fanon, *The Wretched of the Earth*, trans. C. Farrington, New York: Grove Press, 1965, p. 205 (see opening epigraph).

29 US polling companies reduce class categories to

income level bands, ignoring the relation of class to work, control and property ownership.

30 See D. Harvey, *The Enigma of Capital and the Crises of Capitalism*, London: Profile, 2010.

31 For this reason, in the Anglosphere class composition analysis is often referred to as autonomism or autonomist Marxism.

32 See S. Wright, *Storming Heaven: Class Composition and Struggle in Italian Autonomist Marxism*, London: Pluto, 2002.

33 Taylorism and scientific management both refer to techniques developed by Frederick Taylor to increase 'efficiency' by breaking down the work process into a series of standardized operations.

34 M. Tronti, 'Lenin in England', in Red Notes (eds), *Working-Class Autonomy and the Crisis*, London: Red Notes, 1970.

35 S. Bologna, 'Class Composition and the Theory of the Party at the Origins of the Workers' Council Movement', *Telos*, 13 (1972), pp. 4–27.

36 G. Hanlon, *The Dark Side of Management: A Secret History of Management Theory*, London: Routledge, 2016.

37 Comte de Lautréamont, *Maldoror (Le Chants de Maldoror)*, trans. G. Wernham, New York: New Directions, 1965, p. 339 (see opening epigraph).

Chapter 2 Generation Left (Behind)

1 P. Mason, *Post-Capitalism: A Guide to Our Future*, Harmondsworth: Penguin, 2015, p. 3.

2 See B. Bernanke, *The Courage to Act: A Memoir of a Crisis and Its Aftermath*, New York: W. W. Norton & Company, 2015, and A. Darling, *Back from the Brink: 1,000 Days at Number 11*, London: Atlantic Books, 2011.

3 For a vivid telling of this moment see M. Taibbi, 'Secrets and Lies of the Bailout', *Rolling Stone*, 4 January 2013: https://www.rollingstone.com/politics/news/secret-and-lies-of-the-bailout-20130104.

4 Laura Basu has forensically traced the shift in UK media discourse: see L. Basu, *Media Amnesia: Rewriting the Economic Crisis*, London: Pluto, 2018.

5 Oxfam, *Reward Work, Not Wealth*, Briefing Paper, January 2018: https://www.oxfam.org/en/research/reward-work-not-wealth.

6 Oxfam, *An Economy for the 99%: It's Time to Build a Human Economy That Benefits Everyone, Not Just the Privileged Few*, Briefing Paper, January 2017: https://policy-practice.oxfam.org.uk/publications/an-economy-for-the-99-its-time-to-build-a-human-economy-that-benefits-everyone-620170.

7 L. Gardiner, Resolution Foundation press release, 15 March 2017: https://www.resolutionfoundation.org/media/press-releases/unemployment-hits-41-year-low-but-britains-short-lived-pay-recovery-is-rapidly-coming-to-an-end/.

8 In the UK, for instance, research shows that the discourse of intergenerational tension between Baby Boomers and Millennials only took off in 2014. See K. A. Shaw, *Baby Boomers versus Millennials: Rhetorical Conflicts and Interest-Construction in the*

New Politics of Intergenerational Fairness, SPERI report, January 2018: http://speri.dept.shef.ac.uk/wp-content/uploads/2018/01/Baby-Boomers-versus-Milennials-Kate-Alexander-Shaw.pdf.

9 W. Davies, 'The New Neoliberalism', *New Left Review*, 101 (2016), pp. 121–34.

10 For a detailed account of the formation of what Philip Mirowski calls 'the Neoliberal Thought Collective' and its imperviousness to critique, see P. Mirowski, *Never Let a Serious Crisis Go to Waste: How Neoliberalism Survived the Financial Meltdown*, London: Verso, 2013.

11 M. Fisher, *Capitalist Realism: Is There No Alternative?*, Winchester: Zero Books, 2009.

12 This link between material security and working-class confidence makes social democracy an inherently unstable system. See M. Kalecki, 'Political Aspects of Full Employment', *Political Quarterly*, 14(4) (1943), pp. 322–30.

13 On this Left generation gap see S. Hall, *Selected Political Writings: The Great Moving Right Show and Other Essays*, London: Lawrence & Wishart, 1989.

14 S. Huntington, M. Crozier and J. Watanuki, *The Crisis of Democracy: Report on the Governability of Democracies to the Trilateral Commission*, New York: New York University Press, 1975, p. 157.

15 These proposals ranged from the participatory ethic of 1968, through the cybernetic-inflected democracy of Salvador Allende's Project Cybersyn in Chile, to the Medina plan of the Swedish Social Democrats.

16 M. Fisher, *k-punk: The Collected and Unpublished Writings of Mark Fisher (2004–2016)*, London Repeater, 2018, p. 754.

17 K. Sarachild, 'Consciousness-Raising: A Radical Weapon', in Redstockings (eds), *Feminist Revolution*, New York: Random House, 1978.

18 B. C. Gibney, *A Generation of Sociopaths: How the Baby Boomers Betrayed America*, New York: Hachette Books, 2017.

19 See R. Freeman, 'The Great Doubling: The Challenge of the New Global Labor Market', in J. Edwards, M. Crain and A. L. Kalleberg (eds), *Ending Poverty in America: How to Restore the American Dream*, New York: The New Press, 2007.

20 Davies, 'The New Neoliberalism', p. 127.

21 Ibid.

22 M. Fisher and J. Gilbert, 'Capitalist Realism and Neoliberal Hegemony: A Dialogue', *New Formations*, 80/81 (2013), p. 90.

23 For more on this see A. Kotsko, *Why We Love Sociopaths: A Guide to Late Capitalist Television*, Winchester: Zero Books, 2012, p. 42.

24 See M. Foucault, *The Birth of Biopolitics: Lectures at the Collège de France, 1978–1979*, trans. G. Burchell, Basingstoke: Palgrave Macmillan, 2008.

25 We might not become convinced of that idea ourselves, but we start to believe that this reductive model of the human is what everyone else believes.

26 The 'dead yet still dominant' quote, from Neil Smith, 'The Revolutionary Imperative', *Antipode*, 41(s1) (2010), is cited in Davies, 'The New Neoliberalism',

p. 123, which indicates a certain compatibility between our arguments.

27 Brown, *Undoing the Demos*, pp. 33–4.

28 M. Lazzarato, *Signs and Machines: Capitalism and the Production of Subjectivity*, trans. J. D. Jordan, New York: Semiotext(e), 2014, p. 53.

29 For an elaboration of this argument see M. Lazzarato, *Governing by Debt*, trans. J. D. Jordan, New York: Semiotext(e), 2013.

30 J. M. Silva, *Coming Up Short: Coming of Age in the Risk Society*, Oxford: Oxford University Press, p. 10.

31 Ibid., p. 19.

32 Ibid., p. 21.

33 Ibid., p. 142.

Chapter 3 Generation Explosion

1 Mannheim, 'The Problem of Generations', p. 306.

2 Ibid.

3 C. Robin, *The Reactionary Mind: Conservatism from Edmund Burke to Sarah Palin*, Oxford: Oxford University Press, 2013, p. 4.

4 A. R. Zolberg, 'Moments of Madness', *Politics and Society*, 2(2) (1972), p. 183.

5 Ibid., p. 193.

6 Ibid., p. 183.

7 Lazzarato, *Signs and Machines*, p. 147.

8 The concept of a moment of excess was developed by The Free Association, a writing collective in which I was involved. For more, see The Free Association,

Moments of Excess: Movements, Protest and Everyday Life, Oakland, CA: PM Press, 2011.

9 Zolberg, 'Moments of Madness', p. 206.

10 Wu Ming 1, 'We Are All February of 1917', UNC Global Education Center, Chapel Hill, NC, 5 April 2011, p. 8: https://www.wumingfoundation.com/WM1_UNC_talk_on_revolution.pdf.

11 As Althusser might have said, we need to read these events symptomatically, that is, for the gaps and silences that structure them.

12 K. Marx, 'The Eighteenth Brumaire of Louis Bonaparte' (1852), in *Karl Marx and Frederick Engels: Selected Works*, London: Lawrence & Wishart, 1968, p. 97.

13 Ibid.

14 Gilles Deleuze, *Difference and Repetition*, trans. P. Patton, London: Continuum, 2001, p. 92.

15 Marx, 'Eighteenth Brumaire', p. 100.

16 Turkey and Brazil saw a new wave of related protests in 2013, while the French Nuit Debout protests of 2016 also took on the prominent protest repertoire of the 2011 wave.

17 Seeds for Change, 'Consensus Decision-Making': https://theanarchistlibrary.org/library/seeds-for-change-consensus-decision-making.

18 Indeed, as Andrew Cornell shows, the organization that did most to develop and spread a consensus decision-making process in the US, the Movement for a New Society, was acutely aware of these shortcomings and eventually dissolved its organization partly because its attachment to the consensus process

hindered its strategic development. A. Cornell, *Oppose and Propose!* Oakland, CA: AK Press, 2011.

19 P. Gerbaudo, *The Mask and the Flag: Populism, Citizenism and Global Protest*, London: Hurst, 2017, p. 181.

20 See http://wearethe99percent.tumblr.com/.

21 See Silva, *Coming Up Short*.

22 M. Lazzarato, *The Making of the Indebted Man*, New York: Semiotext(e), 2012, p. 134.

23 Q. Norton, 'A Eulogy for #Occupy', *Wired Magazine*, 12 December 2012: http://www.wired.com/opinion/2012/12/a-eulogy-for-occupy/all/.

24 'Real Democracy Now!' was the slogan of the 15M.

25 Norton, 'A Eulogy for #Occupy'.

26 Strike Debt were most famous for buying up and forgiving medical debt purchased on the secondary debt market for cents on the dollar. For further information see http://strikedebt.org/

27 A. Colau and A. Alemany, *Mortgaged Lives: From the Housing Bubble to the Right to Housing*, trans. M. Teran and J. Fuquay, Los Angeles/Leipzig/London: Journal of Aesthetics & Protest Press, 2012, p. 92.

Chapter 4 The Electoral Turn

1 This anecdote was also used in an article I co-wrote as part of the writing collective The Free Association. You can read that article here: http://www.freelyassociating.org/up-we-rise/.

2 K. Ovendon, *Syriza: Inside the Labyrinth*, London: Pluto, 2015, p. 153.

3 R. Nunes, *Spain: From Networks to Parties . . . and Back*, Plan C, 1 June 2015: https://www.weareplanc. org/blog/spain-from-networks-to-parties-and-back/.

4 The idea of a Third Way Left is most closely associated with the governments of Tony Blair in the UK and Bill Clinton in the US, who embraced what Will Davies (in 'The New Neoliberalism') calls normative neoliberalism.

5 M. Reston and G. Ramirez, 'Hillary Clinton Splits Younger, Older Democrat Women', CNN Politics, 10 June 2016: https://edition.cnn.com/2016/06/10/ politics/hillary-clinton-women-generational-divide/ index.html.

6 Labour's good showing in the 2017 election caused some commentators to reassess the appeal of Corbyn's message and a few more leftist pundits were booked on rolling news. However, the quick return to bad-faith hostility by most Third Way columnists shows there's a phenomenon to be explained.

7 Quoted in C. Cadwallader, 'The New Left: Don't Call Them Corbynistas', *The Observer*, 18 September 2016.

8 N. Cohen, 'Labour Conference? More Like the Cult of Saint Jeremy', *The Observer*, 1 October 2017.

9 H. Freeman, 'From Labour's Hard Left to Donald Trump, It's Been the Summer of Personality Cults', *The Guardian*, 30 July 2016.

10 R. Nunes, 'Geração, acontecimento, perspectiva', *Nueva Sociedad*, December 2014.

11 'And what is the phantom fuzz screaming from Chicago to Berlin, from Mexico City to Paris? "We

are REAL REAL REAL!!! as this NIGHTSTICK!" as they feel, in their dim animal way, that reality is slipping away from them.' William Burroughs, commenting on the police beating protesters at the Democratic convention, Chicago, 1968: W. Burroughs, 'The Coming of the Purple Better One', in A. Charters (ed.), *The Portable Sixties Reader*, London: Penguin, 2003, p. 246 (originally from *Esquire*, 1 November 1968).

12 W. Brown, 'Resisting Left Melancholy', *boundary 2*, 26(3) (1999), p. 19.

13 Ibid., p. 26.

14 Ibid., p. 20.

15 Ibid., p. 21.

16 For more on this idea see K. Milburn, 'On Social Strikes and Directional Demands', Plan C, 7 May 2015: https://www.weareplanc.org/blog/on-social-strikes-and-directional-demands/.

17 N. Srnicek and A. Williams, *Inventing the Future: Postcapitalism and a World Without Work*, London: Verso, 2015, p. 169.

18 John McDonnell, the UK's Shadow Chancellor of the Exchequer, has frequently referred to his own strategy as being 'in and against the State'.

19 Mannheim, 'The Problem of Generations', p. 308.

Chapter 5 Reinventing Adulthood

1 M. Hardt and A. Negri, *Assembly*, Oxford: Oxford University Press, 2017, p. 101.

2 D. Losurdo, *Liberalism: A Counter-History*, London: Verso, 2011.

3 For a history of the discourse around a 'property-owning democracy' see B. Jackson, 'Property-Owning Democracy: A Short History': http://www-users. york.ac.uk/~mpon500/pod/Jackson.pdf.

4 Hardt and Negri, *Assembly*, p. 101.

5 Office for National Statistics (2016), *Statistical Bulletin: Marriages in England and Wales: 2015*, 2018: https://www.ons.gov.uk/peoplepopulationand community / birthsdeathsandmarriages / marriageco habitationandcivilpartnerships / bulletins / marriages inenglandandwalesprovisional/2015.

6 K. Johnson, '2.1 Million More Childless US Women Than Anticipated', 12 December 2017: https://carsey. unh.edu/publication/snapshot/more-childless-us-women.

7 Howker and Malik (*Jilted Generation*, p. 57) report that in the UK 'up to 2.8 million people aged between 18 and 44 … report delaying children because they can't obtain affordable housing, while 7 per cent of adults aged between 18 and 30 are delaying marriage because they can't afford to buy a home'.

8 Figures from J. Cribb, A. Hood and J. Hoyle, 'IFS Report: The Decline of Homeownership among Young Adults', 16 February 2018: https://www.ifs. org.uk/publications/10506.

9 Ibid.

10 Others have also noticed that the neoliberal model of adulthood is broken. See K. Crawford, 'Adult Responsibility in Insecure Times', *Soundings*, 41 (2009), pp. 45–55.

11 For more on the invention of youth see J. Savage, *Teenage: The Creation of Youth*, London: Chatto & Windus, 2007.

12 Hardt and Negri, *Assembly*, p. 187.

13 Networks become more valuable the more people interact on them. Currently, the benefits of our interaction are privatized into the coffers of the platform robber barons.

14 See K. Milburn and B. Russell, 'What Can an Institution Do? Towards Public–Common Partnerships and a New Common-Sense', *Renewal*, 26(4), 2018.

15 On universal basic services see J. Portes, H. Reed and A. Percy, *Social Prosperity for the Future: A Proposal for Universal Basic Services*, Institute for Global Prosperity, UCL, 2017: https://www.ucl. ac.uk/bartlett/igp/sites/bartlett/files/universal_basic_ services_-_the_institute_for_global_prosperity_. pdf. For a collection of resources on universal basic income see https://basicincome.org/basic-income/.

16 Hardt and Negri, *Assembly*, p. 100.

17 Ibid., p. 102.

18 For more on how collective practices of care can set the conditions of a new exercise of force, see Milburn, 'On Social Strikes and Directional Demands'.

19 On the super-therapeutic as 'something more than just fixing people up, repairing some of the damage done by daily life under advanced capitalism so that they can get on with their lives', but 'which might have those effects but also go beyond them, enabling people to become extraordinarily empowered

precisely by enhancing their capacity for productive relationships with others', see J. Gilbert, 'Psychedelic Socialism', *openDemocracy*: https://www.opendemo cracy.net/jeremy-gilbert/psychedelic-socialism.